Constructing
a Life Philosophy

Opposing Viewpoints®

Other Books of Related Interest

Constructing
a Life Philosophy

Opposing Viewpoints®

Mary E. Williams, *Book Editor*

Bruce Glassman, *Vice President*
Bonnie Szumski, *Publisher*
Helen Cothran, *Managing Editor*

OPPOSING
VIEWPOINTS®
SERIES

GREENHAVEN PRESS
An imprint of Thomson Gale, a part of The Thomson Corporation

Detroit • New York • San Francisco • San Diego • New Haven, Conn.
Waterville, Maine • London • Munich

LIBRARY OF CONGRESS CATALOGING-IN-PUBLICATION DATA

Constructing a life philosophy / Mary E. Williams, book editor.
    p. cm. — (Opposing viewpoints series)
Includes bibliographical references and index.
    ISBN 0-7377-2927-9 (lib. : alk. paper) — ISBN 0-7377-2928-7 (pbk. : alk. paper)
    1. Life. I. Williams, Mary E., 1960– . II. Opposing viewpoints series (Unnumbered)
BD431.C663 2005
128—dc22
                                                  2004060861

Printed in the United States of America

> "Congress shall make no law...abridging the freedom of speech, or of the press."

First Amendment to the U.S. Constitution

The basic foundation of our democracy is the First Amendment guarantee of freedom of expression. The Opposing Viewpoints Series is dedicated to the concept of this basic freedom and the idea that it is more important to practice it than to enshrine it.

Contents

Why Consider Opposing Viewpoints?

"The only way in which a human being can make some approach to knowing the whole of a subject is by hearing what can be said about it by persons of every variety of opinion and studying all modes in which it can be looked at by every character of mind. No wise man ever acquired his wisdom in any mode but this."

John Stuart Mill

In our media-intensive culture it is not difficult to find differing opinions. Thousands of newspapers and magazines and dozens of radio and television talk shows resound with differing points of view. The difficulty lies in deciding which opinion to agree with and which "experts" seem the most credible. The more inundated we become with differing opinions and claims, the more essential it is to hone critical reading and thinking skills to evaluate these ideas. Opposing Viewpoints books address this problem directly by presenting stimulating debates that can be used to enhance and teach these skills. The varied opinions contained in each book examine many different aspects of a single issue. While examining these conveniently edited opposing views, readers can develop critical thinking skills such as the ability to compare and contrast authors' credibility, facts, argumentation styles, use of persuasive techniques, and other stylistic tools. In short, the Opposing Viewpoints Series is an ideal way to attain the higher-level thinking and reading skills so essential in a culture of diverse and contradictory opinions.

In addition to providing a tool for critical thinking, Opposing Viewpoints books challenge readers to question their own strongly held opinions and assumptions. Most people form their opinions on the basis of upbringing, peer pressure, and personal, cultural, or professional bias. By reading carefully balanced opposing views, readers must directly confront new ideas as well as the opinions of those with whom they disagree. This is not to simplistically argue that everyone who reads opposing views will—or should—change his or her opinion. Instead, the series enhances readers' understanding of their own views by encouraging confrontation with opposing ideas. Careful examination of others' views can lead to the readers' understanding of the logical inconsistencies in their own opinions, perspective on why they hold an opinion, and the consideration of the possibility that their opinion requires further evaluation.

Evaluating Other Opinions

To ensure that this type of examination occurs, Opposing Viewpoints books present all types of opinions. Prominent spokespeople on different sides of each issue as well as well-known professionals from many disciplines challenge the reader. An additional goal of the series is to provide a forum for other, less known, or even unpopular viewpoints. The opinion of an ordinary person who has had to make the decision to cut off life support from a terminally ill relative, for example, may be just as valuable and provide just as much insight as a medical ethicist's professional opinion. The editors have two additional purposes in including these less known views. One, the editors encourage readers to respect others' opinions—even when not enhanced by professional credibility. It is only by reading or listening to and objectively evaluating others' ideas that one can determine whether they are worthy of consideration. Two, the inclusion of such viewpoints encourages the important critical thinking skill of objectively evaluating an author's credentials and bias. This evaluation will illuminate an author's reasons for taking a particular stance on an issue and will aid in readers' evaluation of the author's ideas.

It is our hope that these books will give readers a deeper understanding of the issues debated and an appreciation of the complexity of even seemingly simple issues when good and honest people disagree. This awareness is particularly important in a democratic society such as ours in which people enter into public debate to determine the common good. Those with whom one disagrees should not be regarded as enemies but rather as people whose views deserve careful examination and may shed light on one's own.

Thomas Jefferson once said that "difference of opinion leads to inquiry, and inquiry to truth." Jefferson, a broadly educated man, argued that "if a nation expects to be ignorant and free . . . it expects what never was and never will be." As individuals and as a nation, it is imperative that we consider the opinions of others and examine them with skill and discernment. The Opposing Viewpoints Series is intended to help readers achieve this goal.

David L. Bender and Bruno Leone,
Founders

Greenhaven Press anthologies primarily consist of previously published material taken from a variety of sources, including periodicals, books, scholarly journals, newspapers, government documents, and position papers from private and public organizations. These original sources are often edited for length and to ensure their accessibility for a young adult audience. The anthology editors also change the original titles of these works in order to clearly present the main thesis of each viewpoint and to explicitly indicate the opinion presented in the viewpoint. These alterations are made in consideration of both the reading and comprehension levels of a young adult audience. Every effort is made to ensure that Greenhaven Press accurately reflects the original intent of the authors included in this anthology.

Introduction

"Our work is not so much to find a teacher as to improve our own receptivity and sharpen our ability to hear the teachings all around us."

—David A. Cooper

All around us, significances, meanings, discoveries beckon. To notice them, we must be open, alert, and hospitable. Invariably, meaning resides within the perceiver as well as in what is perceived. As psychologist Alice O. Howell contends, "What we are looking for on earth and in earth and in ourselves is the process that can unlock for us the mystery of meaningfulness in our daily lives. We can only see half of anything. The other half is the meaning we give to what we see.... In every tree, apple, flower, there is an *aha!* waiting!" The process of unlocking meaning is the central focus of this volume. The selections included here offer various "keys" to assist readers as they ask questions about meaning and the values and principles that should guide their lives.

While a book like this is published to meet several needs, three goals were dominant in its creation: first, to kindle curiosity about philosophy, religion, and ethics; second, to assist readers who are developing their own personal goals and conclusions about the meaning of life; and third, to inform readers about philosophies, belief systems, and values that may not be familiar to them. Each chapter addresses these goals in different ways.

The first chapter invites readers to take a deeper look at their current worldview. For example, M. Scott Peck, the author of the first selection, compares our view of reality to a map that we use to negotiate the terrain of life. In conscious and unconscious ways, Peck contends, we all construct our own individual maps, but we have a tendency to cling to the old, outdated maps that served us in our childhood or youth. He encourages readers to confront the changes that life brings by continually revising their maps—a task which, he admits, demands courage and persistence. The other viewpoints in this chapter also draw attention to the fact that we are all encumbered with biases and preconceptions, and authors challenge readers to carefully reexamine their current beliefs and assumptions. In essence, this first chapter highlights the importance of having an open mind, the value of reason, and the necessity of curiosity—the first step toward wisdom.

The book's last four chapters present a view of the maps that people of various philosophies and belief systems have constructed. The insights they contain are pertinent to readers who are wondering: What do I really believe? How should I live my life? What religious or philosophical principles should guide me? The ideas presented in these chapters form a mosaic of philosophies that represent the thinking of atheists as well as believers, skeptics and optimists, rationalists and romantics, scientists and mystics. For example, Richard Robinson, in chapter two, expresses the opinion that this life is all there is and that humanity's finest accomplishment is to live with courage as it awaits its final extinction. On the other hand, in chapter three, Donald E. Miller describes a philosophy built on the conviction that life culminates in a union with a transcendent truth, which he believes is symbolized as God. Although a volume like this is necessarily limited in the number and scope of ideas it can impart, it can serve as a catalyst for further study and reflection.

Even for those who feel certain about their own personal philosophy of life, this book is valuable in that it offers an opportunity to gain a greater awareness of the beliefs held by others. Often our attitudes about unfamiliar philosophies, spiritual disciplines, or moral priorities have been shaped by misinformation, prejudice, or ignorance. For our own personal edification as well as for the benefit of our increasingly interdependent world, it is important to enhance our understanding of the opinions and motives of others.

Perhaps the process that unlocks meaning is, as the structure of this book suggests, the penchant for asking questions—and to continue to question, even after we think we have the answers. As contemporary philosopher Jacob Needleman has observed: "Questioning makes one open, makes one sensitive, makes one humble. We don't suffer from our questions, we suffer from our answers. Most of the mischief in the world comes from people with answers, not from people with questions." Several of life's big questions are addressed in the following chapters of *Opposing Viewpoints: Constructing a Life Philosophy:* The Importance of Choosing a Life Philosophy, What Reveals Life's Ultimate Meaning? How Do Religions Give Life Meaning? What Motivates Moral Behavior? What Principles Should Guide Our Lives? This anthology gives readers an engaging overview of humanity's perennial investigation into the meaning of life.

CHAPTER 1

The Importance of Choosing a Life Philosophy

Chapter Preface

According to the Greek philosopher Socrates, one of the most noble accomplishments in life is for an individual to "know thyself." As the following chapter suggests, it is also one of the most challenging tasks because humans, like all creatures, have limitations. With our tendency to deceive ourselves, to seek comfort, and to avoid painful realities, the search for truth and self-awareness requires serious effort and courage. The authors in this chapter discuss what hinders and helps people in their quest for knowledge, personal growth, and commendable living.

In the first viewpoint renowned author and psychiatrist M. Scott Peck compares our understanding of the world to a "map" that we use to find our way through life. In other words, our view of reality guides us in our decision-making processes, in our life choices, and in our search for meaning. The problem, according to Peck, is that our maps are often inaccurate. People may cling to small and limited maps—outmoded views of reality—that were effective during childhood but not later in life. He maintains that we need to continually adjust our maps to accord with new truths that we encounter throughout our lives. Too often, however, we deceive ourselves because an honest examination of our lives and our problems can be painful. Peck believes that we must face this pain if we are dedicated to finding the truth.

In the second viewpoint the ancient philosopher Plato illustrates why humans tend to resist the work of adjusting their "maps." In his famous allegorical dialogue, he reveals how people too quickly accept the world as it first appears to them. We often believe that the information we receive through our senses gives us reliable facts about our world, but the truth is that our senses provide a very limited view of reality. Truth, Plato suggests, lies beyond what we are ordinarily able to perceive. Consequently, we must use our reasoning abilities to find a fuller understanding of ourselves and our world.

In the third viewpoint contemporary thinker Sam Keen explains that we need to discover the "myths" that can clarify our lives. Similar to Peck's concept of a life map, Keen defines myth as the dominating story lines that guide our culture, our families, and our individual lives. Keen believes that we must carefully examine the myths in which we are living because they likely contain destructive as well as creative elements. As we come to a more complete understanding of our own personal myth, we can make the adjustments that both Peck and Plato challenge us to make in our lives.

Finally, the fourth viewpoint provides somewhat of a counterpoint to the previous three. Philosophy professor Charles Larmore warns that it is a mistake to believe that life is best lived in accord with a rational plan. In Larmore's opinion, the good things in life often come to us unexpectedly and have nothing to do with our own reasoning. While he does not believe that planning is pointless, he argues that the best choice of action lies somewhere between taking charge of our lives and letting life happen to us.

While Larmore questions the idea that the good life comes to us through planning and reasoning, he likely agrees with the other authors that we should avoid the temptation of accepting the world around us at simple face value. All of the authors in the following chapter invite us to seek the truth, a challenge that requires us to examine our most basic assumptions about ourselves and our world.

> *"Our view of reality is like a map with which to negotiate the terrain of life. If the map is true and accurate, we will generally know where we are."*

Choosing a Map for Life

M. Scott Peck

In the viewpoint that follows, M. Scott Peck compares the individual's view of reality to a map that is used to navigate through life. An accurate map provides solid guidance, but an incorrect map causes people to lose their way. Unfortunately, Peck argues, many people do not put enough effort into refining their views of reality; their maps remain small and inaccurate and thus they often hold on to narrow and outmoded ideas well into adulthood. Revising a map—that is, honestly facing the truth about reality and about one's life experiences—can be painful, but it is a necessary part of genuine human growth, Peck concludes. Peck, a contemporary psychiatrist and author, is best known for his 1978 book *The Road Less Traveled*, from which this viewpoint is excerpted.

As you read, consider the following questions:

1. Why do life maps need continual revision, in Peck's opinion?
2. How does the author define transference?
3. In Peck's view, why do many people avoid a life of genuine self-examination?

Truth is reality. That which is false is unreal. The more clearly we see the reality of the world, the better equipped we are to deal with the world. The less clearly we see the reality of the world—the more our minds are befuddled by falsehood, misperceptions and illusions—the less able we will be to determine correct courses of action and make wise decisions.

Map of Life

Our view of reality is like a map with which to negotiate the terrain of life. If the map is true and accurate, we will generally know where we are, and if we have decided where we want to go, we will generally know how to get there. If the map is false and inaccurate, we generally will be lost.

While this is obvious, it is something that most people to a greater or lesser degree choose to ignore. They ignore it because our route to reality is not easy. First of all, we are not born with maps; we have to make them, and the making requires effort. The more effort we make to appreciate and perceive reality, the larger and more accurate our maps will be. But many do not want to make this effort. Some stop making it by the end of adolescence. Their maps are small and sketchy, their views of the world narrow and misleading. By the end of middle age most people have given up the effort. They feel certain that their maps are complete and their Weltanschauung [worldview, or assumptions] is correct (indeed, even sacrosanct), and they're no longer interested in new information. It is as if they are tired. Only a relative and fortunate few continue until the moment of death exploring the mystery of reality, ever enlarging and refining and redefining their understanding of the world and what is true.

Revising Life's Map

But the biggest problem of map-making is not that we have to start from scratch, but that if our maps are to be accurate we have to continually revise them. The world itself is constantly changing. Glaciers come, glaciers go. Cultures come, cultures go. There is too little technology, there is too much technology. Even more dramatically, the vantage point from which we view the world is constantly and quite rapidly changing. When we are children we are dependent, power-less. As adults we may be powerful. Yet in illness or an infirm old age we may become powerless and dependent again. When we have children to care for, the world looks different from when we have none; when we are raising infants, the world seems different from when we are raising adolescents. When we are poor, the world looks different from when we are rich. We are daily bombarded with new information as to the nature of reality. If we are to incorporate this infor-mation, we must continually revise our maps, and sometimes when enough new information has accumulated, we must make very major revisions. The process of making revisions, particularly major revisions, is painful, sometimes excruciat-ingly painful. And herein lies the major source of many of the ills of mankind.

What happens when one has striven long and hard to de-velop a working view of the world, a seemingly useful, work-able map, and then is confronted with new information sug-gesting that that view is wrong and the map needs to be largely redrawn? The painful effort required seems frighten-ing, almost overwhelming. What we do more often than not, and usually unconsciously, is to ignore the new information. Often this act of ignoring is much more than passive. We may denounce the new information as false, dangerous, heretical, the work of the devil. We may actually crusade against it, and even attempt to manipulate the world so as to make it con-form to our view of reality. Rather than try to change the map, an individual may try to destroy the new reality. Sadly, such a person may expend much more energy ultimately in defending an outmoded view of the world than would have been required to revise and correct it in the first place.

This process of active clinging to an outmoded view of re-ality is the basis for much mental illness. Psychiatrists refer to it as transference. There are probably as many subtle varia-tions of the definition of transference as there are psychia-trists. My own definition is: Transference is that set of ways of perceiving and responding to the world which is developed in childhood and which is usually entirely appropriate to the childhood environment (indeed, often life-saving) but which is *inappropriately* transferred into the adult environment.

Examples of Transference

The ways in which transference manifests itself, while always pervasive and destructive, are often subtle. Yet the clearest examples must be unsubtle. One such example was a patient whose treatment failed by virtue of his transference. He was a brilliant but unsuccessful computer technician in his early thirties, who came to see me because his wife had left him, taking their two children. He was not particularly unhappy to lose her, but he was devastated by the loss of his children, to whom he was deeply attached. It was in the hope of regaining them that he initiated psychotherapy, since his wife firmly stated she would never return to him unless he had psychiatric treatment. Her principal complaints about him were that he was continually and irrationally jealous of her, and yet at the same time aloof from her, cold, distant, uncommunicative and unaffectionate. She also complained of his frequent changes of employment. His life since adolescence had been markedly unstable. During adolescence he was involved in frequent minor altercations with the police, and had been jailed three times for intoxication, belligerence, "loitering," and "interfering with the duties of an officer." He dropped out of college, where he was studying electrical engineering, because, as he said, "My teachers were a bunch of hypocrites, hardly different from the police." Because of his brilliance and creativeness in the field of computer technology, his services were in high demand by industry. But he had never been able to advance or keep a job for more than a year and a half occasionally being fired, more often quitting after disputes with his supervisors, whom he described as "liars and cheats, interested only in protecting their own ass." His most frequent expression was "You can't trust a goddam soul." He described his childhood as "normal" and his parents as "average." In the brief period of time he spent with me, however, he casually and unemotionally recounted numerous instances during childhood in which his parents had let him down. They promised him a bike for his birthday, but they forgot about it and gave him something else. Once they forgot his birthday entirely, but he saw nothing drastically wrong with this since "they were very busy." They would promise to do things with him on weekends, but then were usually "too busy." Numerous times they forgot to pick him up from meetings or parties because "they had a lot on their minds."

What happened to this man was that when he was a young child he suffered painful disappointment after painful disappointment through his parents' lack of caring. Gradually or suddenly—I don't know which—he came to the agonizing realization in mid-childhood that he could not trust his parents. Once he realized this, however, he began to feel better, and his life became more comfortable. He no longer expected things from his parents or got his hopes up when they made promises. When he stopped trusting his parents the frequency and severity of his disappointments diminished dramatically.

The Need to Examine Our Childhood Mind-Set

At age four or five . . . [as] we begin to socialize, we internalize the values of family, peer group, religion, ethnic group, nationality, race, gender, and sexual orientation. The combination of [the following] two forces—the drive for happiness (in the form of security and survival, affection and esteem, and power and control), and overidentification with the particular group to which we belong—greatly complicates our emotional programs for happiness. In our younger days, this development is normal. As adults, activity arising from such motivation is childish. . . .

Our emotional programs are filtered through our temperamental biases. . . . If we have an aggressive temperament and like to dominate as many events and people as possible, that drive increases in proportion to the felt privations of that need that we suffered in early childhood. Without facing these early childhood [experiences] and trying to dismantle or moderate them through the exercise of reason . . . they continue to exert enormous influence throughout life.

Thomas Keating, *The Human Condition*, 1999.

Such an adjustment, however, is the basis for future problems. To a child his or her parents are everything; they represent the world. The child does not have the perspective to see that other parents are different and frequently better. He assumes that the way his parents do things is the way that things are done. Consequently the realization—the "reality"—that this child came to was not "I can't trust my parents" but "I can't trust people." Not trusting people therefore became the map with which he entered adolescence and adulthood. With this map and with an abundant store of resentment resulting from his many disappointments, it was inevitable that he came into conflict with authority figures—police, teachers, employers. And these conflicts only served to reinforce his feeling that people who had anything to give him in the world couldn't be trusted. He had many opportunities to revise his map, but they were all passed up. For one thing, the only way he could learn that there were some people in the adult world he could trust would be to risk trusting them, and that would require a deviation from his map to begin with. For another, such relearning would require him to revise his view of his parents—to realize that they did not love him, that he did not have a normal childhood and that his parents were not average in their callousness to his needs. Such a realization would have been extremely painful. Finally, because his distrust of people was a realistic adjustment to the reality of his childhood, it was an adjustment that worked in terms of diminishing his pain and suffering. Since it is extremely difficult to give up an adjustment that once worked so well, he continued his course of distrust, unconsciously creating situations that served to reinforce it, alienating himself from everyone, making it impossible for himself to enjoy love, warmth, intimacy and affection. He could not even allow himself closeness with his wife; she, too, could not be trusted. The only people he could relate with intimately were his two children. They were the only ones over whom he had control, the only ones who had no authority over him, the only ones he could trust in the whole world.

When problems of transference are involved, as they usually are, psychotherapy is, among other things, a process of map-revising. Patients come to therapy because their maps are clearly not working. But how they may cling to them and fight the process every step of the way! Frequently their need to cling to their maps and fight against losing them is so great that therapy becomes impossible. . . .

Truth Can Overcome Transference

The problem of transference is not simply a problem between parents and children, husbands and wives, employers and employees, between friends, between groups, and even between nations. It is interesting to speculate, for instance, on the role that transference issues play in international affairs. Our national leaders are human beings who all had childhoods and childhood experiences that shaped them. What map was Hitler following, and where did it come from? What map were American leaders following in initiating, executing and maintaining the war in Vietnam? Clearly it was a map very different from that of the generation that succeeded theirs. In what ways did the national experience of the Depression years contribute to their map, and the experience of the fifties and sixties contribute to the map of the younger generation? If the national experience of the thirties and forties contributed to the behavior of American leaders in waging war in Vietnam, how appropriate was that experience to the realities of the sixties and seventies? How can we revise our maps more rapidly?

Truth or reality is avoided when it is painful. We can revise our maps only when we have the discipline to overcome that pain. To have such discipline, we must be totally dedicated to truth. That is to say that we must always hold truth, as best we can determine it, to be more important, more vital to our self-interest, than our comfort. Conversely, we must always consider our personal discomfort relatively unimportant and, indeed, even welcome it in the service of the search for truth. Mental health is an ongoing process of dedication to reality at all costs.

What does a life of total dedication to the truth mean? It means, first of all, a life of continuous and never-ending stringent self-examination. We know the world only through our relationship to it. Therefore, to know the world, we must not only examine it but we must simultaneously examine the examiner. . . .

Examination of the world without is never as personally painful as examination of the world within, and it is certainly because of the pain involved in a life of genuine self-examination that the majority steer away from it. Yet when one is dedicated to the truth this pain seems relatively unimportant—and less and less important (and therefore less and less painful) the farther one proceeds on the path of self-examination.

Accepting the Challenge

A life of total dedication to the truth also means a life of willingness to be personally challenged. The only way that we can be certain that our map of reality is valid is to expose it to the criticism and challenge of other map-makers. Otherwise we live in a closed system—within a bell jar, to use [poet] Sylvia Plath's analogy, rebreathing only our own fetid air, more and more subject to delusion. Yet, because of the pain inherent in the process of revising our map of reality, we mostly seek to avoid or ward off any challenges to its validity. To our children we say, "Don't talk back to me, I'm your parent." To our spouse we give the message, "Let's live and let live. If you criticize me, I'll be a bitch to live with, and you'll regret it." To their families and the world the elderly give the message, "I am old and fragile. If you challenge me I may die or at least you will bear upon your head the responsibility for making my last days on earth miserable." To our employees we communicate, "If you are bold enough to challenge me at all, you had best do so very circumspectly indeed or else you'll find yourself looking for another job."

The tendency to avoid challenge is so omnipresent in human beings that it can properly be considered a characteristic of human nature. But calling it natural does not mean it is essential or beneficial or unchangeable behavior. It is also natural to defecate in our pants and never brush our teeth. Yet we teach ourselves to do the unnatural until the unnatural becomes itself second nature. Indeed, all self-discipline might be defined as teaching ourselves to do the unnatural. . . .

For individuals and organizations to be open to challenge, it is necessary that their maps of reality be *truly* open for inspection. . . . It means a continuous and never-ending process of self-monitoring to assure that our communications—not only the words that we say but also the way we say them—invariably reflect as accurately as humanly possible the truth or reality as we know it.

Such honesty does not come painlessly. The reason people lie is to avoid the pain of challenge and its consequences. . . .

We lie, of course, not only to others but also to ourselves. The challenges to our adjustment—our maps—from our own consciences and our own realistic perceptions may be every bit as legitimate and painful as any challenge from the public . . . which is why most people opt for a life of very limited honesty and openness and relative closedness, hiding themselves and their maps from the world. It is easier that way. Yet the rewards of the difficult life of honesty and dedication to the truth are more than commensurate with the demands. By virtue of the fact that their maps are continually being challenged, open people are continually growing people.

> "*[Imagine] human beings living in an underground den.*"

Living with Shadows in a Cave

Plato

Plato (c. 427–347 B.C.) was born into an aristocratic Athenian family and became the most well-known student of Socrates, whom he immortalized in his philosophical essays. Plato eventually founded the Academy, a school that endured for nearly one thousand years and that continues to influence the fields of ethics, philosophy, and theology. In the following allegorical dialogue, excerpted from *The Republic*, Plato illustrates his belief that humans are separated from true reality by their subjective impressions of the world. People tend to accept their sensory perceptions as accurate representations of fact, Plato points out, but human senses only give a distorted reflection, or shadow, of reality. The unreliability of sensory experience means that people must carefully use reason as a tool to examine their beliefs.

As you read, consider the following questions:

1. According to Plato, what happens first when a prisoner in the cave is released from his bonds?
2. Once the prisoner has become accustomed to the light of the outside world, what feelings does he have about his fellow prison-mates, in Plato's opinion?
3. Once the released prisoner returns to the underground den, what do the other prisoners conclude about his experience, according to Plato?

Plato, *The Republic*, translated by Benjamin Jowett, 1894.

And now, I said, let me show in a figure how far our nature is enlightened or unenlightened:—Behold! human beings living in an underground den, which has a mouth open towards the light and reaching all along the den; here they have been from their childhood, and have their legs and necks chained so that they cannot move, and can only see before them, being prevented by the chains from turning round their heads. Above and behind them a fire is blazing at a distance, and between the fire and the prisoners there is a raised way; and you will see, if you look, a low wall built along the way, like the screen which marionette players have in front of them, over which they show the puppets.

I see.

Strange Prisoners

And do you see, I said, men passing along the wall carrying all sorts of vessels, and statues and figures of animals made of wood and stone and various materials, which appear over the wall? Some of them are talking, others silent.

You have shown me a strange image, and they are strange prisoners.

Like ourselves, I replied; and they see only their own shadows, or the shadows of one another, which the fire throws on the opposite wall of the cave?

True, he said; how could they see anything but the shadows if they were never allowed to move their heads?

And of the objects which are being carried in like manner they would only see the shadows?

Yes, he said.

And if they were able to converse with one another, would they not suppose that they were naming what was actually before them?

Very true.

And suppose further that the prison had an echo which came from the other side, would they not be sure to fancy when one of the passers-by spoke that the voice which they heard came from the passing shadow?

No question, he replied.

To them, I said, the truth would be literally nothing but the shadows of the images.

That is certain.

Release of the Prisoners

And now look again, and see what will naturally follow if the prisoners are released and disabused of their error. At first, when any of them is liberated and compelled suddenly to stand up and turn his neck round and walk and look towards the light, he will suffer sharp pains; the glare will distress him, and he will be unable to see the realities of which in his former state he had seen the shadows; and then conceive some one saying to him, that what he saw before was an illusion, but that now, when he is approaching nearer to being and his eye is turned towards more real existence, he has a clearer vision—what will be his reply? And you may further imagine that his instructor is pointing to the objects as they pass and requiring him to name them,—will he not be perplexed? Will he not fancy that the shadows which he formerly saw are truer than the objects which are now shown to him?

Far truer.

And if he is compelled to look straight at the light, will he not have a pain in his eyes which will make him turn away to take refuge in the objects of vision which he can see, and which he will conceive to be in reality clearer than the things which are now being shown to him?

True, he said.

Leaving the Cave

And suppose once more, that he is reluctantly dragged up a steep and rugged ascent, and held fast until he is forced into the presence of the sun himself, is he not likely to be pained and irritated? When he approaches the light his eyes will be dazzled, and he will not be able to see anything at all of what are now called realities.

Not all in a moment, he said.

He will require to grow accustomed to the sight of the upper world. And first he will see the shadows best, next the reflections of men and other objects in the water, and then the objects themselves; then he will gaze upon the light of the moon and the stars and the spangled heaven; and he will see the sky and the stars by night better than the sun or the light of the sun by day?

Certainly.

Last of all he will be able to see the sun, and not mere reflections of him in the water, but he will see him in his own proper place, and not in another; and he will contemplate him as he is.

Certainly.

He will then proceed to argue that this is he who gives the season and the years, and is the guardian of all that is in the visible world, and in a certain way the cause of all things which he and his fellows have been accustomed to behold?

The Cave

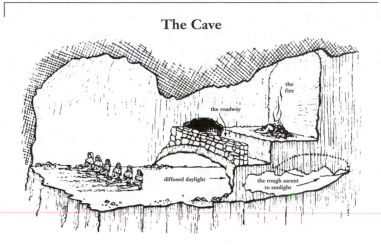

The Great Dialogues of Plato, Warmington and Rouse, eds.

Clearly, he said, he would first see the sun and then reason about him.

And when he remembered his old habitation, and the wisdom of the den and his fellow prisoners, do you not suppose that he would felicitate himself on the change, and pity them?

Certainly, he would.

And if they were in the habit of conferring honors among themselves on those who were quickest to observe the passing shadows and to remark which of them went before, and which followed after, and which were together; and who were therefore best able to draw conclusions as to the future, do you think that he would care for such honors and glories, or envy the possessors of them? Would he not say with Homer, "Better to be the poor servant of a poor master," and to endure anything, rather than think as they do and live after their manner?

Yes, he said, I think that he would rather suffer anything than entertain these false notions and live in this miserable manner.

Returning to the Cave

Imagine once more, I said, such a one coming suddenly out of the sun to be replaced in his old situation; would he not be certain to have his eyes full of darkness?

To be sure, he said.

And if there were a contest, and he had to compete in measuring the shadows with the prisoners who had never moved out of the den, while his sight was still weak, and before his eyes had become steady (and the time which would be needed to acquire this new habit of sight might be very considerable), would he not be ridiculous? Men would say of him that up he went and down he came without his eyes; and that it was better not even to think of ascending; and if any one tried to loose another and lead him up to the light, let them only catch the offender, and they would put him to death.

No question, he said.

Conclusion

This entire allegory, I said, you may now append, dear Glaucon, to the previous argument; the prison house is the world of sight, the light of the fire is the sun, and you will not misapprehend me if you interpret the journey upwards to be the ascent of the soul into the intellectual world according to my poor belief, which, at your desire, I have expressed—whether rightly or wrongly God knows. But, whether true or false, my opinion is that in the world of knowledge the idea of good appears last of all, and is seen only with an effort; and, when seen, is also inferred to be the universal author of all things beautiful and right, parent of light and of the lord of light in this visible world, and the immediate source of reason and truth in the intellectual; and that this is the power upon which he who would act rationally either in public or private life must have his eye fixed.

"We gain personal authority and power in the measure that we . . . discover and create a personal myth that illuminates and informs us."

Discovering Our Personal Myth

Sam Keen

Sam Keen is a former professor of philosophy and religion and a former contributing editor of *Psychology Today*. He is currently a lecturer, consultant, and author who has written more than a dozen books on myth, spirituality, and self-improvement. The following viewpoint is taken from his preface to *Your Mythic Journey*, a book he coauthored with educator and writer Anne Valley-Fox. In this excerpt, Keen discusses the significance of myth, which he defines as the combination of customs, traditions, stories, and philosophies that form each individual's understanding of life. Keen argues that it is important for people to discover the myth that has shaped their lives so that they can consciously update it, retaining what is beneficial, rejecting what is harmful, and adding new ideas gleaned from personal experience.

As you read, consider the following questions:

1. How is myth commonly defined, according to Keen, and how does this popular definition differ from the author's definition?
2. In what way can the inherent conservatism of myth be destructive, in the author's opinion?
3. According to Keen, how can individuals gain personal authority and power?

Sam Keen, "Preface," *Your Mythic Journey*, by Sam Keen and Anne Valley-Fox. Los Angeles, CA: Jeremy P. Tarcher, 1989. Copyright © 1989 by Sam Keen and Anne Valley-Fox. Reproduced by permission in the USA by Penguin Group (USA) Inc., 345 Hudson St., New York, NY 10014. In the UK by permission of Sam Keen.

It seems that Americans are finally taking seriously what Carl Jung, the Swiss psychologist, said is the most important question we can ask ourselves: "What myth are we living?"...

What Is a Myth?

What is a myth? Few words have been subject to as much abuse and been as ill-defined as *myth*. Journalists usually use it to mean a "lie," "fabrication," "illusion," "mistake," or something similar. It is the opposite of what is supposedly a "fact," of what is "objectively" the case, and of what is "reality." In this usage myth is at best a silly story and at worst a cynical untruth. Theologians and propagandists often use myth as a way of characterizing religious beliefs and ideologies other than their own.

Such trivialization of the notion of myth reflects false certainties of dogmatic minds, an ignorance of the mythic assumptions that underlie the commonly accepted view of "reality," and a refusal to consider how much our individual and communal lives are shaped by dramatic scenarios and "historical" narratives that are replete with accounts of the struggle between good and evil empires: our godly heroes versus the demonic enemy.

In a strict sense *myth* refers to "an intricate set of interlocking stories, rituals, rites, and customs that inform and give the pivotal sense of meaning and direction to a person, family, community, or culture." A living myth, like an iceberg, is 10 percent visible and 90 percent beneath the surface of consciousness. While it involves a conscious celebration of certain values, which are always personified in a pantheon of heroes (from the wily Ulysses to the managing [former CEO of Chrysler Corporation] Lee Iacocca) and villains (from the betraying Judas to the barbarous [president of Libya] Moammar Kadafi), it also includes the unspoken consensus, the habitual way of seeing things, the unquestioned assumptions, the automatic stance. It is differing cultural myths that make cows sacred objects for Hindus and hamburger meals for Methodists, or turn dogs into pets for Americans and roasted delicacies for the Chinese.

At least 51 percent of the people in a society are not self-consciously aware of the myth that informs their existence. Cultural consensus is created by an unconscious conspiracy to consider the myth "the truth," "the way things *really* are." In other words, a majority is made up of literalists, men and women who are not critical or reflective about the guiding "truths"—myths—of their own group. To a tourist in a strange land, an anthropologist studying a tribe, or a psychologist observing a patient, the myth is obvious. But to the person who lives within the mythic horizon, it is nearly invisible.

For instance, most Americans would consider potlatch feasts, in which Northwest Indian tribes systematically destroy their wealth, to be irrational and mythic but would consider the habit of browsing in malls and buying expensive things we do not need (conspicuous consumption) to be a perfectly reasonable way to spend a Saturday afternoon. To most Americans the Moslem notion of *jihad*—holy war—is a dangerous myth. But our struggle against "atheistic communism" is a righteous duty. Ask a born-again Christian about the myth of the atonement, and you will be told it is no myth at all but a revealed truth. Ask a true believer of Marxism about the myth of the withering away of the state, and you will get a long explanation about the "scientific" laws of the dialectic of history.

I suggest two analogies that may help to counteract the popular trivialized notion of myth. The dominant myth that informs a person or a culture is like the "information" contained in DNA or the program in the systems disk of a computer. Myth is the software, the cultural DNA, the unconscious information, the metaprogram that governs the way we see "reality" and the way we behave.

Myths Can Be Creative or Destructive

The organizing myth of any culture functions in ways that may be either creative or destructive, healthful or pathological. By providing a world picture and a set of stories that explain why things are as they are, it creates consensus, sanctifies the social order, and gives the individual an authorized map of the path of life. A myth creates the plotline that organizes the diverse experiences of a person or a community into a single story.

But in the same measure that myth gives us security and identity, it also creates selective blindness, narrowness, and rigidity because it is intrinsically conservative. It encourages us to follow the faith of our fathers, to hold to the time-honored truths, to imitate the way of the heroes, to repeat the formulas and rituals in exactly the same way they were done in the good old days. As long as no radical change is necessary for survival, the status quo remains sacred, the myth and ritual are unquestioned, and the patterns of life, like the seasons of the year, repeat themselves. But when crisis comes— a natural catastrophe, a military defeat, the introduction of a new technology—the mythic mind is at a loss to deal with novelty. As [educator] Marshall McLuhan said, it tries to "walk into the future looking through a rearview mirror."

Families Have Myths

Every family, like a miniculture, also has an elaborate system of stories and rituals that differentiate it from other families. The Murphys, being Irish, understand full well that Uncle Paddy is a bit of a rogue and drinks a tad too much. The Cohens, being Jewish, are haunted each year at Passover when they remember the family that perished in the Holocaust. The Keens, being Calvinists, are predestined to be slightly more righteous and right than others, even when they are wrong. And within the family each member's place is defined by a series of stories. Obedient to the family script, Jane, "who always was very motherly even as a little girl," married young and had children immediately, while Pat, "who was a wild one and not cut out for marriage," sowed oat after oat before finding fertile ground.

Family myths, like those of the Kennedy clan, may give us an impulse to strive for excellence and a sense of pride that helps us endure hardship and tragedy. Or they may, like the myths of alcoholic or abusive families, pass a burden of guilt, shame, and failure from generation to generation as abused children, in turn, become abusive parents, ad nauseam. The sins, virtues, and myths of the fathers are passed on to the children of future generations.

Every Individual Has a Personal Myth

Finally, the entire legacy and burden of cultural and family myth comes to rest on the individual. Each person is a repository of stories. To the degree that any one of us reaches toward autonomy, we must begin a process of sorting through the trash and treasures we have been given, keeping some and rejecting others. We gain the full dignity and power of our persons only when we create a narrative account of our lives, dramatize our existence, and forge a coherent personal myth that combines elements of our cultural myth and family myth with unique stories that come from our experience. As my friend David Steere once pointed out to me, the common root of "authority" and "authorship" tells us a great deal about power. Whoever authors your story authorizes your actions. We gain personal authority and power in the measure that we question the myth that is upheld by "the authorities" and discover and create a personal myth that illuminates and informs us.

What [philosopher] George Santayana said about cultures is equally true for individuals: "Those who do not remember history are condemned to repeat it." If we do not make the effort to become conscious of our personal myths gradually, we become dominated by what psychologists have variously called repetition compulsion, autonomous complexes, engrams, routines, scripts, games. One fruitful way to think of neurosis is to consider it a tape loop, an oft-told story that we repeat in our inner dialogues with ourselves and with others. "Well, I'm just not the kind of person who can . . ." "I never could . . ." "I wouldn't think of . . .". While personal myths give us a sense of identity, continuity and security, they become constricting and boring if they are not revised from time to time. To remain vibrant throughout a lifetime we must always be inventing ourselves, weaving new themes into our life-narratives, remembering our past, re-visioning our future, reauthorizing the myth by which we live.

| *"The idea that life should be the object of a plan is false to the human condition."*

Challenging the Idea of a Life Plan

Charles Larmore

In the following viewpoint Charles Larmore challenges the notion that people will live a good life by following the precepts of a rational plan. This idea of controlling one's life through reason and planning has been espoused by ancient and modern philosophers, but human experience reveals that happiness is often the result of unanticipated events, Larmore points out. Moreover, the good that people pursue often falls short of the good that happens to them unexpectedly. While there is nothing wrong with organizing and shaping one's life, people should also recognize that unforeseen experiences will challenge their plans and enhance their lives in unpredictable ways. Larmore is a professor of political science and philosophy at the University of Chicago.

As you read, consider the following questions:
1. According to Larmore, what was one of the main themes of Marcel Proust's *Remembrance of Things Past?*
2. Between what two extremes does the good life lie, in the author's opinion?
3. How does being passive contribute to living a good life, in Larmore's view?

Charles Larmore, "The Idea of a Life Plan," *Social Philosophy & Policy*, vol. 16, Winter 1999, pp. 96–98. Copyright © 1999 by Cambridge University Press. Reproduced by permission.

When philosophers undertake to say what it is that makes life worth living, they generally display a procrustean habit of thought which the practice of philosophy itself does much to encourage. As a result, they arrive at an image of the human good that is far more controversial than they suspect. The canonical view among philosophers ancient and modern has been, in essence, that the life lived well is the life lived in accord with a rational plan. To me this conception of the human good seems manifestly wrong. The idea that life should be the object of a plan is false to the human condition. It misses the important truth which [French writer Marcel] Proust, by contrast, discerned and made into one of the organizing themes of his great meditation on disappointment and revelation, *A la recherche du temps perdu* [*Remembrance of Things Past*]. The happiness that life affords is less often the good we have reason to pursue than the good that befalls us unexpectedly.

The mistake to which I refer has molded the way that philosophy on the whole has dealt with the most fundamental question we ask ourselves, the question of how we are to live our lives. I do not believe that there has been anything inevitable about this development, anything inherent in the philosophical enterprise that has led to the mistaken ideal of a life plan. It is not the very nature of philosophy which is to blame, for philosophy really has no essence beyond the goal of comprehensive understanding, and that may mean a great many things. But I am convinced that philosophers have by and large proceeded on the wrong track in dealing with this question, and that their error is more than accidental, stemming as it does from what has been one of their abiding preoccupations.

Do We Really Lead Our Lives?

Before explaining this point further, I should indicate what precisely I believe is wrong in the idea of a life plan. The mistake lies at its very core, in the basic attitude toward life to which it gives expression. That attitude is the view that a life is something we are to lead and not something we should allow to happen to us. We flourish as human beings, it supposes, only if we shape our lives ourselves, instead of leaving them to be the hostages of circumstance and whim. If this is our outlook, then we should obviously seek to live in accord with some unified conception of our overall purposes and of the ways to achieve them. In other words, we should devise for ourselves some "plan of life" at least in its broad strokes, if not fine-tuned in its smallest details. To the extent that we work out our plan in a rational way, giving due weight to our beliefs about what is valuable, our knowledge of our own abilities, and our grasp of the possibilities the world provides, we will have determined the character of our good and the way to achieve it. Success is not guaranteed, of course; but we will have done the best we could.

What Life Gives Us

In exchange for what our imagination leads us to expect and which we vainly give ourselves so much trouble to try to discover, life gives us something which we were very far from imagining.

Marcel Proust, *Albertine Disparue*, 1925.

This conception of life seems perhaps so sensible that we may wonder what could be amiss. The rub, I am inclined to say, is that it is too sensible. But no doubt the better and more straightforward way to put the objection is by observing that this frame of mind embodies too great a timidity in the face of the power that experience has to change our sense of what makes life worth living. Its guiding assumption is that we should take charge of our lives, bringing them under our rule as best we can. And yet we go wrong in making so much of a contrast between leading a life and letting life happen to us. The good lies between these two extremes. It belongs to a life that is not just led but met with as well, a life that is both self-directed and shaped from without. We miss an important aspect of what gives our lives meaning, when we suppose that we live well by living in accord with an all-embracing plan of our own devising. The happy life spans, not just the good we plan for, but also the unlooked-for good which befalls us.

The basis of my opposition to the idea of a life plan is not, I should observe, the age-old perception that the best-laid schemes of mice and men go oft awry. Our plans, when we put them into practice, certainly risk defeat at the hands of reality. And disappointment may seem inescapable when so complicated a matter as life itself is made the object of a plan. Many people have raised this sort of difficulty, none perhaps so movingly as Samuel Johnson in *Rasselas* (published in 1759). In this novel, the young prince Rasselas, cloyed by his pampered existence in the Happy Valley, escapes to make his own way in the world. His faith is that with experience will come the ability to make, as he says, the proper "choice of life." But Imlac, his tutor, tries to disabuse him of this hope. Our grasp of how the world is put together is too unreliable for any such choice to stand a real chance of success. "The causes of good and evil," Imlac insists,

> are so various and uncertain, so often entangled with each other, so diversified by various relations, and so much subject to accidents which cannot be foreseen that he who would fix his condition upon incontestable reasons of preference, must live and die inquiring and deliberating. . . . Very few live by choice. Every man is placed in his present condition by causes which acted without his foresight, and with which he did not always willingly cooperate.

There is considerable wisdom in these observations, but they do not really suffice to undermine the idea of a life plan. Snarled and unpredictable though the ways of the world may be, we can set our sights on ends whose achievement seems minimally imperiled by chance or misfortune. To choose our purposes with an eye to lessening the likelihood of frustration has been, after all, the almost universal advice of the philosophical tradition, the grounds on which it has often elevated, for example, the life of virtue above the pursuit of more fickle goods such as honor or wealth. Probably no way of life can escape altogether the play of luck. But the fragility of whatever good we may achieve is not the point I am concerned to make.

My protest against the idea of a life plan is of a different and more fundamental kind. It arises not from the precariousness of our plans, but rather from the drawbacks of planning. A significant dimension of the human good escapes us if we believe that our attitude toward life must be at bottom one of foresight and control, as the idea of a life plan entails.

Let Beauty Surprise You

Beauty is a free spirit and will not be trapped within the grid of intentionality. . . .

The wonder of the Beautiful is its ability to surprise us. With swift, sheer grace, it is like a divine breath that blows the heart open. Immune to our strategies, it can take us when we least expect it. Because our present habit of mind is governed by the calculus of consumerism and busyness, we are less and less frequently available to the exuberance of beauty. Indeed, we have brought calculation to such a level that it now seems unsophisticated to admit surprise.

John O'Donohue, *Beauty: The Invisible Embrace*, 2004.

On the contrary, we live well when we are not simply active, but passive too. There is an openness to life's surprises which we do well to maintain. For the unexpected can turn out to be, not just the mishap that defeats our plans, but also the revelation that discloses new vistas of meaning, new forms of happiness and understanding which we least suspected or never imagined and which may change our lives and who we are in the deepest way. Sometimes we then learn that we have been mistaken in the things we have hitherto had reason to value. Other times we find simply that we must add a new element to our notion of our good (though the addition often ends up affecting the complexion of our other commitments as well). . . .

Life Is Unruly

Life is too unruly to be the object of a plan, and again not simply because our schemes may founder when applied. Obviously, we often fail to achieve the good we pursue. But more important and certainly more neglected by philosophy is the happy fact that the good we pursue, the good we have reason to pursue, is bound to fall short of the good that life has yet to reveal. From this insight we should not infer that the nature of the good life is a question not worth trying to answer since every answer will prove inadequate. It is natural to think about what elements go into making up our good, and my remarks have not been meant to deny that each of us lives, or ought to live, with an idea in mind of the good life. The target of my criticism has been the view that any such idea must be of a life we have taken charge of and brought under the rule of our own purposes. The good life is not, I have argued, the life lived in accord with a rational plan. It is the life lived with a sense of our dual nature as active and passive beings, bent on achieving the goals we espouse, but also liable to be surprised by forms of good we never anticipated. A life lived in the light of this more complex ideal can accommodate, it can even welcome, the way in which an unexpected good may challenge our existing projects. We will not thereby avoid being surprised (nor should we want to), but we will know enough not to be surprised at being surprised.

Nothing I have said should suggest, either, that planning is wrong or pointless. Prudence is an undeniable virtue, and not solely in the handling of the little things of life. We cannot hope to live well if we do not direct ourselves toward achieving goals which have a ramifying significance, which organize our various activities and give our lives meaning. But we err if we suppose that prudence is the supreme virtue and that the good life is one which unfolds in accord with a rational plan.

CHAPTER 2

What Reveals Life's Ultimate Meaning?

Chapter Preface

Philosophers, sages, theologians, and scientists have responded to the question "Why is there something rather than nothing?" in various ways. For example, some existentialist philosophers contend that such a question is unanswerable, and that one should ask instead "What should we do with this 'something' in which we live?" For them, life's meaning rests in the freedom to choose—a freedom that entails commitment and responsibility but that avoids an unquestioning reliance on commonly accepted beliefs. Many religious believers, on the other hand, maintain that human existence results from the creative act of a supreme being who cannot be perceived through our senses or our reasoning. They envision life as a divinely conceived path that leads humans from alienation and self-centeredness to some form of salvation or enlightenment. Scientists, however, seek to discover life's mysteries through observable data, precise experimentation, and theoretical speculation. While most scientists agree that science cannot answer the question of *why* the universe exists, it can help us see *how* the universe works and what role humanity plays in it. With the information gleaned from science, humans can shape their future, creating meaning and purpose as they learn and evolve.

The authors in the following chapter present different answers to the question of what reveals life's meaning. Twentieth-century philosopher Richard Robinson argues that there is no ultimate "secret" of the universe and that there is no supreme being. He contends, however, that humans can find meaning in promoting self-chosen virtues and in loving one another as they face their coming extinction. Comparative religion scholar George E. Saint-Laurent discusses how religious believers pursue meaning through communion with the sacred, a mystery that at once permeates and transcends human senses and intellect. Physics instructor Wayne Anderson maintains that the discoveries of science offer a solid intellectual basis for understanding how humans fit into natural and cosmic processes. He believes that science will eventually play a role in usurping religion's reliance on a supreme being for meaning. On the other hand, science writer and editor

Sharon Begley contends that both faith and science provide genuine insights into the mysteries of the universe and the meaning of human life. She suggests that while science and religion respond to the question of meaning in different ways, each can heal the excesses of the other: Science can cleanse religion of its superstition, and religion can rid science of its arrogance.

While these authors may disagree on where life's meaning is to be found, they all share a concern for human welfare and ponder what role humanity plays in the cosmos. Their musings on choice, science, faith, and reason offer fascinating insights relevant to the construction of a life philosophy.

"There is no possibility of 'making sense of the universe', if that means discovering one truth about it which explains everything else about it and also explains itself."

Ultimate Meaning Does Not Exist

Richard Robinson

Richard Robinson (1902–1996) taught philosophy at Cornell University in Ithaca, New York, and at Oxford University in England. In the following viewpoint, excerpted from his book *An Atheist's Values*, Robinson argues that there is no single truth that can explain the existence of the universe and no god that will rescue humanity from disasters and death. Given these circumstances, humans should accept their predicament and face their future with courage, cheerfulness, and dignity. Since humans are alone in the universe, Robinson contends, their most noble and life-affirming choice is to pursue goodness, truth, and human solidarity.

As you read, consider the following questions:

1. Why are humans permanently insecure, in Robinson's opinion?
2. In the author's view, why is atheism more noble than theism?
3. According to Robinson, why do humans need to create new ceremonies?

Richard Robinson, *An Atheist's Values*. Oxford, UK: Blackwell, 1975. Copyright © 1975 by Blackwell Publishers. Reproduced by permission.

The human situation is this. Each one of us dies. He ceases to pulse or breathe or move or think. He decays and loses his identity. His mind or soul or spirit ends with the ending of his body, because it is entirely dependent on his body.

The human species too will die one day, like all species of life. One day there will be no more men. This is not quite so probable as that each individual man will die; but it is overwhelmingly probable all the same. It seems very unlikely that we could keep the race going forever by hopping from planet to planet as each in turn cooled down. Only in times of extraordinary prosperity like the present could we ever travel to another planet at all.

We are permanently insecure. We are permanently in danger of loss, damage, misery, and death.

Our insecurity is due partly to our ignorance. There is a vast amount that we do not know, and some of it is very relevant to our survival and happiness. It is not just one important thing that we can ascertain and live securely ever after. That one important thing would then deserve to be called 'the secret of the universe'. But there is no one secret of the universe. On the contrary, there are inexhaustibly many things about the universe that we need to know but do not know. There is no possibility of 'making sense of the universe', if that means discovering one truth about it which explains everything else about it and also explains itself. Our ignorance grows progressively less, at least during periods of enormous prosperity like the present time; but it cannot disappear, and must always leave us liable to unforeseen disasters.

The main cause of our insecurity is the limitedness of our power. What happens to us depends largely on forces we cannot always control. This will remain so throughout the life of our species, although our power will probably greatly increase.

There Is No God

There is no god to make up for the limitations of our power, to rescue us whenever the forces affecting us get beyond our control, or provide us hereafter with an incorruptible haven of absolute security. We have no superhuman father who is perfectly competent and benevolent as we perhaps once supposed our actual father to be.

Bouthillier. © 2003 by Art Bouthillier. Reproduced by permission.

What attitude ought we to take up, in view of this situation? It would be senseless to be rebellious, since there is no god to rebel against. It would be wrong to let disappointment or terror or apathy or folly overcome us. It would be wrong to be sad or sarcastic or cynical or indignant. . . .

Cheerfulness is part of courage, and courage is an essential part of the right attitude. Let us not tell ourselves a comforting tale of a father in heaven because we are afraid to be alone, but bravely and cheerfully face whatever appears to be the truth.

Theism Versus Atheism

The theist sometimes rebukes the pleasure-seeker by saying: *We were not put here to enjoy ourselves: man has a sterner and nobler purpose than that.* The atheist's conception of man is, however, still sterner and nobler than that of the theist. According to the theist we were put here by an all-powerful and all-benevolent god who will give us eternal victory and happiness if we only obey him. According to the atheist our situation is far sterner than that. There is no one to look after us but ourselves, and we shall certainly be defeated.

As our situation is far sterner than the theist dares to think, so our possible attitude towards it is far nobler than he conceives. When we contemplate the friendless position of man in the universe, as it is right sometimes to do, our attitude should be the tragic poet's affirmation of man's ideals of behaviour. Our dignity, and our finest occupation, is to assert and maintain our own self-chosen goods as long as we can, those great goods of beauty and truth and virtue. And among the virtues it is proper to mention in this connection above all the virtues of courage and love. There is no person in this universe to love us except ourselves; therefore let us love one another. The human race is alone; but individual men need not be alone, because we have each other. We are brothers without a father; let us all the more for that behave brotherly to each other. The finest achievement for humanity is to recognize our predicament, including our insecurity and our coming extinction, and to maintain our cheerfulness and love and decency in spite of it. We have good things to contemplate and high things to do. Let us do them.

We need to create and spread symbols and procedures that will confirm our intentions without involving us in intellectual dishonesty. This need is urgent today. For we have as yet no strong ceremonies to confirm our resolves except religious ceremonies, and most of us cannot join in religious ceremonies with a good conscience. When the *Titanic* went down, people sang 'nearer, my God, to thee'. When the Gloucesters were in prison in North Korea they strengthened themselves with religious ceremonies. At present we know no other way to strengthen ourselves in our most testing and tragic times. Yet this way has become dishonest. That is why it is urgent for us to create new ceremonies, through which to find strength without falsehood in these terrible situations. It is not enough to formulate honest and high ideals. We must also create the ceremonies and the atmosphere that will hold them before us at all times. I have no conception how to do this; but I believe it will be done if we try.

"People practice religion in the more or less conscious quest for human significance."

Religion Pursues Life's Meaning

George E. Saint-Laurent

The major world religions pursue answers to questions about humanity's origins, purpose, and future, writes George E. Saint-Laurent in the following viewpoint. Religion also prescribes a way, or path, that guides behavior and that leads to transformation, salvation, or enlightenment. Judaism, Christianity, Islam, Hinduism, and Buddhism all profess that ultimate meaning resides in a sacred dimension or absolute reality that transcends human senses or intellect, the author explains. Each of these religions also teaches that human transformation entails the rejection of a self-centered life and an embracing of the divine will. Saint-Laurent is an emeritus professor of comparative religion and spirituality at California State University in Fullerton.

As you read, consider the following questions:
1. What are "life's great questions," according to Saint-Laurent?
2. According to the author, what do Jews, Christians, and Muslims see as humanity's central problem? How do Hindus and Buddhists define the human predicament?
3. Why is it that theological language can provide only an indirect description of the sacred, in Saint-Laurent's view?

George E. Saint-Laurent, *Spirituality and World Religions: A Comparative Introduction*. Mountain View, CA: Mayfield Publishing Company, 2000. Copyright © 2000 by Mayfield Publishing. Reproduced by permission of McGraw-Hill, Inc.

Religion is a *pursuit*, and religious persons must be prepared to make a sustained effort throughout their life. Religion can be an idyllic search for absolute Truth, Love, and Beauty, but it can also demand a rigorous program of performance. An authentic faith commitment usually engenders a practical way of life and can even create a whole culture, as in the case of medieval Christendom. That is why Moses, the Buddha, Jesus, and Muhammad required that their disciples not only hope in the future but also apply themselves to virtuous conduct here and now. These men were teachers of uncommon vision, but they were also men of action who marshaled all their physical energy and inner resources toward their life's mission.

People practice religion in the more or less conscious quest for human significance. They often feel that they would be troubled, incomplete, and restless without their religion. Religious men and women seek satisfying answers to life's great questions: From where have I come, what does it mean to be a human being, why am I here, and what will happen to me after death? To the extent that practitioners faithfully adhere to the teachings of their tradition, they discover a new meaning in life. Of course, authentic faith should bear fruit in practice. Religious people have a framework of meditation and/or rituals of prayerful worship to purify their intentions and ethical criteria to discipline their activity. Devotees learn to interpret their daily experiences from a perspective of inspiring vision and lasting values. As their spirituality deepens and matures, they often feel a new conviction of purpose and mission, perhaps even a sense of vocation and election "from above."

The Pursuit of Transformation

Religion is the pursuit of *transformation*. Religious people want to integrate harmoniously all the levels of their humanity. They long for liberation from whatever traps and binds them. They seek healing from every scar of past brokenness, elevation to a new dimension of consciousness, and transfiguration according to their new ideal of complete personhood.

Jews, Christians, Muslims, Hindus, and Buddhists all teach a source of meaning not of this world: a confirmation in peace (Hebrew *shalom*, Greek *eirene*, Arabic *salam*, Sanskrit *shanti*, and Pali *santi*). They also agree that we initially find ourselves in a dehumanizing predicament of dis-ease. Human life, indeed, abounds with difficulties of every description, but human life itself is a major problem. That is why, they say, we feel ill at ease and alienated, as though we are strangers who do not quite fit into our own world. That is also why a haunting malaise troubles the most fortunate among us at the radical core of our being: our pervasive obsession with ourselves. We must, they insist, pass over from our systemic egocentricity to become reoriented about a new focal center.

Consequently, each of these world religions presents itself as a secure and trustworthy *way*. Each way is more than an ennobling concept to raise up the heart; it is also a path that guides behavior and a road that leads to salvation. Jews, therefore, speak of "the way of Torah." Early Christians identified themselves as followers of "the way" (*hodos*). Muslims submit to God's will by following the "straight path" (*shariah*) of Islamic religious law. Hindus, with that broad tolerance for which they are famous, present no less than four major "ways" (*margas*) to *moksha* ("liberation"). Buddhists teach the "middle way" (*magga*) to Nibbana (or Nirvana) ("state of being blown out, cool"—that is, liberation from the wheel of rebirth), and some of them refer to each major interpretation of Buddhism as a *yana* ("vehicle").

A Message of Fulfillment

These world religions proclaim ways to personal transformation for those who follow them, despite the affliction of moral evil, physical misery, and death. They announce a message of human fulfillment by which followers may conduct their lives with heartfelt purpose and an uplifting morality by which followers may devote themselves to others with compassionate service. Believers suffer frustrations, disappointments, and failures, of course. Yet each of these religions offers its adherents the strength to pick up the pieces after setbacks, go on in hope, and finally prevail, either within this world or, perhaps, within some further dimension in the future.

Of course, many people are born into a living tradition that nourishes them, and they spontaneously appropriate their parents' religion as their own. Other individuals deliberately choose a particular religion after careful reflection, because it enables them to make sense out of their confusion and wholeness out of their dividedness. They have found its teachings about human dignity and destiny, good and evil, health and pain, life and death to be uniquely persuasive. Both kinds of religious persons confidently root their hopes in a ground that is imperceptible to the senses, yet accessible through faith, enlightenment, or some sort of initiation into a "higher" level of existence. Their own belief system rings true for them and resounds in the deepest recesses of their hearts, while doctrines of other religions appear "less probable."

The Human Predicament

For Jews, Christians, and Muslims, our human problem is the moral ensnarement of *sin* that estranges us from a personal God, but the Creator in faithful and merciful love offers redemption. In Jewish thought, human beings must use their freedom responsibly and make the right choice between two strong inclinations: good tendencies (*yetzer ha tov*) and bad tendencies (*yetzer ha ra*). They must obey the 613 commandments of God's instruction (Torah) in order to confirm their good inclinations and pass from dehumanizing self-will to the ennobling righteousness of God's holy people. In the Christian view, people must struggle against a state of sinfulness that they inherit from their first parents (original sin); they then aggravate this solidarity in sinfulness by their own transgressions (actual, or personal, sins). They must by Christ's assistance and empowerment (grace) die to self and pass over with him to resurrection as God's adopted children. In Islamic understanding, human beings must reject the temptations of the devil (Iblis) and choose freely to surrender (Islam) unreservedly to the will of God (Allah) as God's servants and finally, perhaps, as God's friends.

For Hindus and Buddhists, our predicament is not moral but intellectual: We human beings erroneously fail to see things for what they really are, and so we become trapped by the law of karma (action, consequence of an action) on the wheel of endless rebirth. Hindus identify our difficulty as the illusion of individual separateness, the false sentiment that we

54

are discrete selves in our own right, distinct from one another and from the one universal and absolute Self (Brahman-atman). Hindus insist that we all possess the same Self (atman) and that all selfishness is, in fact, based upon pointless error. Therefore, we must adopt one of the approved *margas* and pass over from the state of error that constrains us in rebirth to a liberating realization of our true identity in the universal Self. Buddhists, on the other hand, view our difficulty as the delusion and ignorance of permanent selfhood as such. This ignorance leads to craving desire, and craving desire causes rebirth to further suffering. In fact, the notion of self, whether individual or universal, is empty and void of any reality. Therefore, we must follow the "middle way," with its Noble Eightfold Path, in order to pass over from our state of ignorance that causes craving desire, rebirth, and suffering to a state of enlightenment and Nibbana. . . .

The Impact of a Sacred Worldview

Religion is the pursuit of transformation under the impact of a sacred worldview. The notion of the sacred is utterly decisive here (although problematical and resistant to discrete analysis), and we must work out at least some general understanding of its meaning. Jews, Christians, Muslims, and Hindus acknowledge the sacred as existing in an ultimate and absolute reality such as God or the Godhead (Brahman-atman). Buddhists recognize the sacred in the ceaseless process or flow of being, although many of them reject any dualistic distinction between the "sacred" and the "profane" (just as the flow of this-worldly experience and absolute Nibbana are really inseparable and the same). All of these religious people further recognize the sacred as an awe-inspiring dimension of whatever symbolizes and/or communicates the *numinous* ("pertaining to the divinely Other"). For example, devotees encounter the numinous in consecrated shrines, seasons of celebration, inspired books, and rites of passage. All religious people experience the sacred as beyond all comprehension, impossible to define, and very difficult to describe. Yet they insist that the sacred is incontestably real, irresistibly attractive, wondrously provocative, and enduringly fascinating. They know that they can approach the sacred only with the utmost reverence.

What Belief Demands

To say "I believe . . . in the creator" proclaims, out of the center of my soul, that I know that life is a gift, a responsibility, a venture into human accountability for which there is no excuse acceptable, no justification adequate enough to explain why I did nothing to complete a world given to me for safe-keeping. We may, of course, fail because failure is also a mark of creaturehood, the beginning of a growth learned over and over again, from generation to generation, until the end of time. Success is, therefore, not required. We are frail, uncertain. But the outpouring through us of the Breath of God, the spirit that brought each of us into being and sustains us there, is of the essence of God's work on earth. The massacres may go on, the injustices may be legalized, the oppressions may be theologized, the barbarisms may be taken for granted everywhere, but I am expected to meet inhumanity with humanity, human darkness with the gleam of the divine eye at all times, spiritual death with the living Breath of God. I am expected to draw from the Being that is the source of my being so that all of us together may someday, somehow grow to full stature, become that from which we were made, be everything that creaturehood demands.

Joan Chittister, *In Search of Belief*, 1999.

The sacred transcends every limitation and overflows every boundary. The whole universe cannot fully contain the sacred and its phenomena, because it exceeds our every ordinary horizon. If the ultimately sacred is a divine being, it may be at once deeply *immanent* (abiding within) and absolutely *transcendent* (exceeding limits, transcending). The God of the Jews, Christians, and Muslims is distinct from all creatures, yet God pervades them all in immanence and surpasses them all in transcendence. For many Hindus, the ultimate divine principle (Brahman-atman), is identified with all things as It pervades them all in immanence and surpasses them all in transcendence. The divinity contains the cosmos, but the cosmos does not contain the divinity.

The Mystery of the Sacred

Since the sacred is intrinsically mysterious, we are incapable of grasping it directly, whether by our senses or by our intellect. Since the sacred exceeds all that we encounter in our natural and ordinary experience, it is *ineffable* (beyond adequate human expression). That is why theological language, for example, can at best be no more than indirect and analogical or negative. Even Thomas Aquinas (1225–74), a philosopher-theologian of extraordinary acumen, affirmed that we know what God is not rather than what God is. Our clouded knowledge of the sacred can be no more than a distant reflection, and our stammering speech about the sacred can be no more than a metaphorical suggestion. Our words may point toward the sacred from afar, but they cannot encompass it. Still, religious people have always tried mentally to probe the meaning of the sacred and have attempted verbally to articulate its significance. They have often created *myths* (vividly imaginative stories) in order to pass on their experience to the next generation. These colorful narratives form the core of their nonwritten and scriptured traditions, creeds, and texts for worshipping communities.

It is very important to realize that religious persons may persevere in their religiosity whether or not they have any emotional feelings in the presence of the sacred. Religion is not essentially a matter of sensibility and sentiment. Some people are certain that they have somehow encountered the sacred, although they have perceived little or nothing on an emotional level. Others may engage themselves with enthusiastic and even passionate commitment to the sacred. Even these people recognize, however, that their faith or enlightenment has to sustain them even when all the sweetness of sensible consolation dissolves into the bitter darkness of aridity.

Most religious persons are not mystics who frequently or habitually experience the sacred as immediately available. Some do speak poetically of savoring the supernal delight of the divine presence or hearing the melody of the divine voice. Others recount how the ecstasy of spiritual betrothal has drawn them up out of themselves into the divine embrace. Nevertheless, the vast majority of religious people lead humdrum lives of unspectacular but faithful practice in an earthbound and uninspired context.

Religious people engage in numerous kinds of activities. For example, they likely pray and worship, meditate upon scriptures, engage in ritual celebrations, fast, give alms, go on pilgrimages, or serve the needy—and maintain some sort of contact with the sacred through it all. They all seek to commune with awe-inspiring Reality, and they hope that their particular way will lead them to final transformation, enlightenment, or salvation.

The defining dimension of all religious exercises is the sacred connection. Buddhists of the Theravada ("teaching of the elders"—that is, the Buddhism of Southeast Asia), for example, deny the existence of both a personal God and a human soul, yet they are certainly religious, since they acknowledge the sacred. Reform Jews are often agnostic in regard to afterlife, but they too are undeniably religious, since they are committed to the sacred. Members of the Society of Friends (Quakers) and practitioners of Zen give no place to ritual, but they are religious beyond doubt, since they pursue communion with the sacred. Moreover, religious traditions differ from one another in their descriptions of the sacred. They may attempt to speak of the sacred literally, figuratively, or mythically—or not at all. In the last analysis, however, the sacred still remains pivotal and indispensable.

"Science does indeed offer mysteries far more profound than those powered by religion and can point to a highly satisfying meaning to life."

Science Can Uncover Life's Meaning

Wayne Anderson

Scientific discovery offers a solid philosophical framework from which to ponder the meaning of life, Wayne Anderson asserts in the following viewpoint. By offering insights into the nature of matter and humanity's place in the cosmos, science provides the intellectual basis that enables humankind to probe the mysteries of the universe without relying on religious belief. In Anderson's opinion, science connects us to the rest of the universe and reveals that we are part of an intricate web of life—not divinely created masters of the planet. This recognition enables us to embrace nature and seek out meaning and purpose as we evolve, he contends. Anderson teaches physics and astronomy at Sacramento City College in Sacramento, California.

As you read, consider the following questions:

1. What is string theory, according to Anderson?
2. In Anderson's opinion, what is one of the major shortcomings of revealed religions?
3. Where may the human sense of morals and of good and evil have stemmed from, according to the author?

Wayne Anderson, "Why Should People Choose Science over Religion?" *Free Inquiry*, vol. 21, Fall 2001, pp. 58–59. Copyright © 2001 by the Council for Democratic and Secular Humanism, Inc. Reproduced by permission.

The most beautiful experience we can have is the mysterious. It is the fundamental emotion which stands at the cradle of true art and true science. Whoever does not know it and can no longer wonder, no longer marvel, is as good as dead, and his eyes are dimmed. It was the experience of mystery—even if mixed with fear—that engendered religion.

—Albert Einstein

Anyone hoping to promote a scientific rather than a religious view of the world absolutely must recognize the extremely valuable and comforting things that religion brings to vast numbers of people. Besides providing a sense of community and moral guidance, religion says there is a meaning to life, and it brings people into contact with the profound mystery of existence. Even in the greatest of tragedies, people find comfort in the belief that someone is in control, even though they do not know his plan. And religion's grappling with the deep mystery of the universe, why it exists and how it came to be, helps to explain why first-rate intellects such as [Isaac] Newton have been so powerfully drawn to it.

What can a scientific view of the world offer people to compete with the comforts bestowed by religion? Can science give meaning to life, and can it envelop people in a sense of deep mystery? I would like to suggest that science does indeed offer mysteries far more profound than those powered by religion and can point to a highly satisfying meaning to life that does not depend on rules laid down by some omnipotent being.

Science and Mystery

In the opening [epigraph], Einstein splendidly captures the sense of awe that accompanies the cutting edge of scientific discovery. The scientist stands in wonder at the incomprehensible majesty of the universe, from the most minute constituents of matter to immense clusters of galaxies to the elegant natural laws that give it all coherence. What are some of these great mysteries of science?

What is matter? The objects of the material world seem so *real*. Yet if we look deeply, this reality begins to fade. The overwhelming majority of each atom—99.9999999999999 percent—is empty space. Probing the protons and neutrons of the atom, we find them also to be nearly total emptiness containing pointlike particles called *quarks*. What, if anything, makes up the quarks? No one knows.[1]

But *why* are there quarks and electrons? Physicists have developed "string theory" to try to explain their existence. According to this idea, the elementary particles arise as vibrations of ten- or eleven-dimensional space-time membranes (called "p-branes"). We do not experience these extra dimensions because they are so tightly curved in on each other that they are beyond our senses. If quarks and electrons have any size at all, it likely comes from the scale of the vibrating p-branes rather than any solid surface. We are left with the disconcerting thought that matter itself may well be an illusion caused by the wiggles of space-time.

What is reality? The Newtonian world of our ordinary senses is a comfortingly rational place. Effect follows cause as time inexorably unfolds. But the deeper realm of quantum mechanics seems an unfathomable mystery. Even in a vacuum, matter pops in and out of existence. Such behavior, called "quantum fluctuations," is not caused by anything, it just happens randomly. Things like electrons are both waves *and* particles. This microscopic world of quantum physics is a supreme mystery. How can we visualize an electron as being both a wave and a particle, or matter fluctuating into and out of existence? Quantum mechanics allows us to calculate observable quantities to astonishing precision, so we must take it seriously, but the view of the physical world that it presents us is really incomprehensible.

Ultimate Questions

Countless people have gazed at the blazing night sky and asked where it all came from and perhaps even *why* there is a universe Such profound questions are at the forefront of modern scientific speculation.

The universe is held together by the four fundamental forces of gravitation, electromagnetism, the weak force, and

---

1. The same is true of the electron. Although it is not made of quarks, its internal structure (if it has any) is presently unknown.

the strong nuclear force. But why these and no others, and where did they come from? Matter everywhere seems to obey the same fundamental laws, but where did these laws come from, and why do they have their particular form? Were they somehow determined by chance at the beginning of the universe, or is there some underlying reason for them? As Einstein said, "What really interests me is whether god had any choice in the creation of the world."

The universe appears to have begun some twelve to fifteen billion years ago—the so-called Big Bang. But *why* did the Big Bang occur? Some astronomers speculate that new universes (or "multiverses") are being created all the time. If so, are the physical laws in them the same as in our multiverse, or are they totally different? And—the most profound mystery of all—why is there a universe in the first place? *Why is there something rather than nothing?*

Can Science Give Our Lives Meaning?

If by "meaning" we expect science to reveal that a superior power is directing our lives, the answer is no. There is no credible evidence for such a guiding force. However, science can show us how we fit into the fabric of the universe. It can reveal how deeply we are embedded in nature, rather than being special creations. Science can provide us with the raw materials—the knowledge—but we human beings must devise our own purpose. Science will not *replace* religion. Rather it will be a major part of the intellectual basis of whatever worldview does replace it. The failure to recognize that humans are indeed a part of nature is one of the great shortcomings of revealed religions.

I would suggest that three branches of science are especially relevant in providing a basis on which to devise meaning for ourselves. These are astronomy, evolutionary biology, and ecological environmentalism.

Astronomy

Astronomy connects us to the rest of the universe. It shows us that we live on a small planet orbiting a middle-aged yellow dwarf star near the outer edge of a spiral galaxy, one of billions of other such galaxies. Armed with such knowledge, it is difficult to think of ourselves as special beings holding central importance in the eyes of some creator.

The Beauty and Power of Science

To discover that the Universe is some 8 to 15 billion and not 6 to 12 thousand years old improves our appreciation of its sweep and grandeur; to entertain the notion that we are a particularly complex arrangement of atoms, and not some breath of divinity, at the very least enhances our respect for atoms; to discover, as now seems probable, that our planet is one of billions of other worlds in the Milky Way Galaxy and that our galaxy is one of billions more, majestically expands the arena of what is possible; to find that our ancestors were also the ancestors of apes ties us to the rest of life and makes possible important—if occasionally rueful—reflections on human nature.

Plainly there is no way back. Like it or not, we are stuck with science. We had better make the best of it. When we finally come to terms with it and fully recognize its beauty and its power, we will find, in spiritual as well as in practical matters, that we have made a bargain strongly in our favor.

Carl Sagan, *Skeptical Inquirer*, March/April 1996.

Astronomy also reveals that we came from the stars. The atoms of our bodies, and everything else on Earth, were fused in the nuclear infernos of generations of stars before our solar system even existed. Near the ends of their lives, these stars blew those atoms out into space, where they mixed with vast gas clouds out of which stars and planets—and us—are born. As Carl Sagan often said, we are stardust. But the story does not end here. About five billion years from now, our sun will swell to become a red giant, expelling some of its matter, including that of the vaporized planets, back into space, there to mix with more gas clouds to continue the cycle of star birth. Not only did we come from the stars, but we will eventually return to the stars.

Lest one think that this is just sterile scientific knowledge, consider the case of a close friend of mine who died of AIDS. As his body was succumbing to the disease, and, as he struggled to accept his approaching death, he explained that he was returning to the universe. He certainly did not welcome his death—neither do religious folk—but he recognized it as part of a vast cosmic cycle. Surely such knowledge makes the end of life easier to accept than fear of eternal torment.

Evolutionary Biology

If astronomy shows us that our atoms were forged in the stars, evolutionary biology tells us how these building blocks came to be shaped into us, by the same process that led to all other living things. We are no special creation, but rather a product of the natural processes that produced the myriad variety of living things on Earth.

But we must not stop with the evolution of our bodies. Not only are our brains a product of natural selection, but according to the emerging field of evolutionary psychology, so are some of the *thoughts* that are formed by those brains. Our morals and our sense of good and evil may have evolved subject to the pressures of natural selection. They are not universal absolutes handed down by a divine being.

Once we accept that our morals may have evolved, we have the dazzling freedom to change them as necessary, without the fear of divine wrath. Although our notions of proper behavior must have had survival value early in our evolution, some of them have lost that value and should be abandoned. An apt case is the vehement religious condemnation of "deviant" sexuality. When making as many babies as possible was vital to the survival of the tribe, it made sense to discourage other sexual outlets. But when we probably have more people than the Earth can comfortably carry and modern medicine ensures the survival of most infants, what is the problem with nonprocreative sex?

Of course many people, even nonreligious ones, find repugnant the notion that there is no absolute good and evil. It seems to open the door to the worst kinds of moral relativism. However, science does seem to be pointing in that direction. As Robin Wright observed in *The Moral Animal*, the truth can make you free, but it may not make you happy. Nevertheless, we do ourselves no good by pretending that the morals of the past carry unassailable authority. If we are to survive in the future, we must be ready to modify our ideas of right and wrong to fit a world vastly different from the one in which we evolved.

Ecological Environmentalism

We share this planet with millions of other life forms, all of which evolved as we did. We were given no special dominion over other life. Yet throughout human history, people treated every single thing on Earth as though it was put here solely for our use. Other species exploit their environment as best they can, but we are much better at it. And therein lies the problem: we are *too* efficient at it.

Sometime near the middle of the twentieth century, human beings began to comprehend fully the enormous extent to which technological society was usurping the Earth. In the past few decades, many of us have come to think of ourselves as participants in, rather than masters of, the intricate web of life on this planet. This view has spread to much of the world and will not go away. We now ask of things like housing developments, scientific projects, and even international treaties: how will this affect the environment? The environment may not always come out on top, but it has become an important player. As human society continues to reform itself, environmentalism will gain even greater importance as a secular principle guiding our choices.

By themselves scientific discoveries do not give humans a purpose in life. But they do anchor us firmly in the natural processes of the universe. They can provide the philosophical and intellectual framework from which to chart our own course through the cosmos. Such a voyage may be terrifying, but it can also be exhilarating!

"In the skies themselves, and in what cosmologists are learning about them, the armies of the mind and the forces of the spirit are searching for common ground."

Both Religion and Science Can Reveal Life's Meaning

Sharon Begley

Science and religion have often clashed, most notably since Charles Darwin published his theory of evolution in the nineteenth century, notes Sharon Begley in the following viewpoint. The scientist's understanding of life as the result of chemical reactions and natural selection seemed to conflict with the religious believer's view of life as a divine creation. By the end of the twentieth century, however, a growing number of specialists were seeing scientists and people of faith engaged in a mutually supportive quest for understanding. Many believe that recent scientific theories point to the existence of an ultimate reality or supreme being and that both science and faith can enhance the human sense of connection to the cosmos. Begley, an award-winning science writer, is a senior editor at *Newsweek* magazine.

As you read, consider the following questions:
1. According to Begley, what is Walt Whitman's complaint in his poem about the "learn'd astronomer"?
2. What conclusions did astronomer Alan Sandage's research lead him to, according to the author?
3. What comment did Albert Einstein, quoted by the author, make about science and religion?

Sharon Begley, "Introduction," *The Hand of God: Thoughts and Images Reflecting the Spirit of the Universe,* edited by Michael Reagan. Kansas City, MO: Andrews McMeel Publishing, 1999. Copyright © 1999 by Lionheart Books, Ltd. Reproduced by permission of Templeton Foundation Press.

The age of naked-eye astronomy has lasted for most of our time on Earth: if the length of humankind's 2.5 million-year tenure is taken as one 24-hour day, then the era of the telescope has lasted a mere 15 seconds. Throughout the other 23 hours, 59 minutes and 45 seconds, our unaided eyes could no more penetrate the veils covering the secrets of the universe than the flash of a firefly could penetrate the canopy of stars that unfurled above us every cloudless night. Few people realized that, beyond the visible stars and moon and occasional planet, there lay worlds and worlds without end. But even though we could see no farther than the frontispiece of the universe, in the years before telescopes the cosmos still drew us. It was the stuff of eternity, infinity—as unbounded as humankind's imagination.

Come, the stars invited; lie supine at the top of a hill on a night when neither the glow of the moon nor a roof of clouds interferes with your view of the sky, in a place where the lights of human habitation are too dim to wash out the view. Look up. There, where the Pleiades burn. Or there—where Orion stretches so boldly over the southern sky. And everywhere, where the uncounted and uncountable hosts prick the black velvet. Look. Stare. Maybe the indifferent heavens will offer a sign, however small, that there is a world beyond the world we see, that there is meaning in the void and a harmony between the mind of man and the limitless reaches of space.

Closing the gaps of that limitless reach have been the 20th century's high-powered telescopes. Namesake of Hubble, remote offspring of Galileo, today's space-based machinery bring us images so far beyond what we could ever imagine that they have changed dramatically our view of the heavens and the origins of the universe. And yet, ironically, the more focused the portraits from deep space, the more meticulous and specific our calculations, the more it seems improbable, even impossible, that our world could have been an arbitrary occurrence.

The majesty of the heavens and their regularity—the cycling of the seasons, the rhythm of day and night—inspire a suspicion that we simply cannot be looking at some meaningless accident. How fitting, then, that it is in cosmology—

the scientific study of the beginning and evolution of the universe—where the stage is set for a historic reconciliation of those two rivals for man's awe: science and religion. In the skies themselves, and in what cosmologists are learning about them, the armies of the mind and the forces of the spirit are searching for common ground.

Science Versus Religion

To appreciate the seismic change taking place in the relationship between science and faith, one need only recall how deeply the rift between the two has become part of our culture. Walt Whitman captured it best when he wrote in the poem that was to become part of *Leaves of Grass*,

> When I heard the learn'd astronomer,
> When the proofs, the figures, were ranged in columns
> before me
> When I was shown the charts and the diagrams, to add,
> divide, and measure them;
> When I, sitting, heard the astronomer, where he lectured
> with much applause in the lecture-room,
> How soon, unaccountable, I became tired and sick;
> Till rising and gliding out, I wander'd off by myself,
> In the mystical moist night-air, and from time to time,
> Look'd up in perfect silence at the stars.

Whitman was not alone when he complained that "the learn'd astronomer's" discoveries had spoiled the mystery and romance of the stars; his poem describes the science most of us know. It is a science that has, traditionally, encroached on the terrain of religion, offering a natural (and often dry) explanation for what had previously been regarded as wondrous and even supernatural. It is a science that obliterates mysteries and replaces them with a differential equation. It is a science that addresses totally different questions than religion: Science explains the world, God is behind the world; science explains what is, religion offers a sense of what ought to be; science tells us how the world acts, religion tells us how we should act.

And yet it was not always so, For most of the previous 2,000 years, science and religion were engaged in a common quest for understanding, each taking strength from the other.

Science as an Avenue to Faith

Until the middle of the 19th century, science was perceived not as antithetical to faith but rather as an avenue to deeper faith and to greater appreciation for the works of the Creator. In nature, scientists believed, could be discerned the handiwork of God.

The leading lights of the Scientific Revolution were men of faith as well as men of science. Early astronomers like Tycho Brahe and Johannes Kepler, devout Christians both, studied the motions of the planets and believed that, in so doing, they were getting a peek at the blueprints that God had drawn for the universe. Isaac Newton did not doubt that in uncovering the laws of motion and universal gravitation, he was being granted a glimpse of the operating manual of the vast machine called Creation that God had assembled and kept running.

These early scientists trusted that their inquiries would yield knowledge because they believed that God had created a rational, ordered world, a world governed by laws and not by chaos or divine whim, a world in which discoveries therefore had universal meaning: if an apple fell *here* for one reason, then that reason applied throughout the universe. The world was not an endless sequence of unique cases. Without the confidence that there existed a consistent, rational, eternal set of principles governing nature, there wouldn't be much point in doing science—whose goal is, after all, the uncovering of the regularities of nature that we have come to call laws.

In the 17th century, science and religion signed a sort of mutual nonaggression treaty, in which each vowed to refrain from spreading into the domain of the other. For science, this move was defensive: by declaring outright that its discoveries did not, and could not, be used as tools to undermine belief, science was declaring that it operated in a domain parallel to rather than overlapping that where religion reigned. This was partly a reaction to how the Church had treated Galileo.[1] If science took the position that its discov-

---

1. In 1616 Italian astronomer Galileo Galilei was placed under lifelong house arrest for supporting the theory of a sun-centered solar system. This theory conflicted with the religious dogma of the time.

eries did not speak to the truth or falsity of religion, there would be no more—or, at least, less excuse for—putting scientists under house arrest. For faith, a nonaggression treaty also offered protection: by asserting that it spoke to realities beyond the reach of science, it effectively inoculated itself from any surprise discoveries that might otherwise be interpreted as undermining its teachings.

The Rise of Science

But the rise of science had already brought with it Copernicus's Sun-centered solar system, which knocked Earth from the center of creation. Next came Newton's physics, which made of the universe an inanimate wind-up machine. The Enlightenment's focus on reason as the supreme human power, its philosophies of reductionism and materialism, and its rejection of authority and revelation and text, were all antithetical to religion. The truce was fraying.

Science and Religion

Science wants to know the mechanism of the universe, religion the meaning. The two cannot be separated. Many scientists feel there is no place in research for discussion of anything that sounds mystical. But it is unreasonable to think we already know enough about the natural world to be confident about the totality of forces.

Charles Townes, physicist, 1964 Nobel Prize winner.

In 1859 Charles Darwin published, in *On the Origin of Species*, his theory of evolutionary biology, which seemed to dethrone the Creator and replace him with blind chance. Darwin more than any scientist before dislodged humans from the apex of the tree of life, making them seem almost incidental to Creation, an afterthought, some meaningless bits of carbon chemistry dotting an insignificant planet orbiting an ordinary star way out in the hinterland of a galaxy indistinguishable from the other 100 billion galaxies believed to fill the universe. The biologist's view of life as a series of complex chemical reactions did not lie easily with the theologian's idea of life as a divine gift; if everything from the creation of the planets to the eruption of a volcano to the leukemia that takes the life of a child is seen as having, in fact or in theory, a natural cause and explanation, then it seemed like there was no room left for God to act in the world. Darwin's theory of evolution through natural selection was arguably the single event that allowed the supposedly unbridgeable chasm between God and science to attain the status of iconic truth.

From the mid-19th century on, the relationship between science and faith deteriorated into one of animosity, at least in the West. True, some theologians made their peace with modern science: one American clergyman welcomed Darwin's theory of evolution through chance and natural selection because that view implied that God had created a world that could and did make itself. This was a gift of love, the clergyman argued, allowing the creation to have independence rather than making it a divine puppet theater. But few men of God saw Darwin's theory in any such positive light. Instead, most other theologians began to identify science as the enemy, as a hostile force invading and laying waste to the sacred. . . .

A Pointless Universe?

With the scythe of science slashing away at all evidence of the divine, no wonder so many people have come to view science as nihilistic, as threatening, as undermining their hope that there is meaning in their lives, as replacing a sense of being unique and God-created with an existential void. This view was famously summed up by Nobel Prize-winning physicist Steven Weinberg, who concluded, "The more the universe seems comprehensible, the more it seems pointless."

Or maybe not. There is another interpretation of the understanding we have achieved. This view holds, contrary to Weinberg, that humankind's very ability to comprehend the universe suggests a profound connection, heretofore lost, between the mind of man and the works of God. Just as science once threatened faith, now it is—at least for some—restoring faith by offering this solace. For others, science is at least serving a function that faith alone once did: making humans feel connected to, not alienated from, creation.

The aspect of science that offers this hope is so basic that it is like [poet Edgar Allan] Poe's purloined letter: right under our noses, we overlook it. This is the remarkable fact that the human mind can do science in the first place—that it can, in other words, figure out the world. Science works. Lights turn on when we flick a switch; buildings stand; water boils when we heat it; planets show up in the predicted place in space when we send robotic emissaries to them.

Why should this be so? "The magic of science is that we can understand at least part of nature—perhaps in principle all of it—using the scientific method of inquiry," says astronomer and physicist Paul Davies, winner of the Templeton Prize for advancing religion. Why, Davies asks, should the laws of nature be comprehensible and accessible to humans? It could, of course, be just a quirk, a coincidence, with no deeper meaning. Or, it could say something purely scientific—though we don't know, precisely, what—about the kind of beings that emerge from nature: as children of what Davies calls "the cosmic order," perhaps it is inevitable that their minds should "reflect that order in their cognitive capabilities."

Some scientists and theologians suspect, however, that the harmony between the intellectual ability of man and the laws of nature reflects something more profound. It need not be anything so simplistic as, "God made the world, and God made me, so He made me able to understand the rest of His Creation." It is, instead, one of those places where a scientific discovery—that the universe can be fathomed by the mind of man—serves a function that, once, only religion could. To wit: a sense of connectedness between humans and the cosmos. . . .

Alan Sandage's Observations

One scientist whose research led him to faith is Alan Sandage, the astronomer who has spent the better part of the past forty years at the great telescopes on Mt. Wilson and Las Campanas Observatories. Sandage inherited the mantle of Edwin Hubble, who in 1929 discovered that the universe is expanding, rushing out like a tide and carrying along with it galaxies and nebulas like so much flotsam and jetsam upon the waves of spacetime. After Hubble's death in 1953, Sandage assumed the task of measuring the fate of the universe.

To do so, Sandage observed two kinds of stars: exploded

stars called supernovas and variable stars called Cepheids, whose period of variation in brightness and intrinsic luminosity are precisely related. Sandage determined the distance to these stars by the shift in their light spectra, and calculated their recession velocity. The relationship between those two numbers would reveal whether the universe would expand forever or, one day, stop and reverse course, hurtling toward a Big Crunch. For the insights they gave him into the design of the cosmos, Sandage called the photographic plates that he and others made at Palomar's telescopes "the plates of Moses."

Tinged with Mysticism

After close on two centuries of passionate struggles, neither science nor faith has succeeded in discrediting its adversary. On the contrary, it becomes obvious that neither can develop normally without the other. And the reason is simple: the same life animates both. Neither in its impetus nor its achievements can science go to its limits without becoming tinged with mysticism and charged with faith.

Pierre Teilhard de Chardin, *The Phenomenon of Man*, 1959.

As much as any other 20th-century astronomer, Sandage actually figured out the Creation: his observations showed how old the universe is (15 billion years or so) and that it is expanding just fast enough to do so forever. But throughout it all Sandage was nagged by mysteries whose answers were not to be found in the glittering supernovas. Among them: Why is there something rather than nothing? He began to despair of answering such questions through reason alone. "It was my science that drove me to the conclusion that the world is much more complicated than can be explained by science," he says. "It is only through the supernatural that I can understand the mystery of existence."

The Mystery of Quantum Mechanics

Some scientists who study not the macro-world of astronomy but the micro-world of particles smaller than an atom have been similarly moved. Quantum mechanics, the branch of physics that describes events at the subatomic level, is a consistent, empirically proved framework that predicts how subatomic particles behave and interact. But it is also "spooky," to use Einstein's description. His most famous experiment in this regard is so odd that, when Einstein devised it with two collaborators as a thought experiment in 1935, he called it a paradox. It goes like this. Let's say that a radioactive atom decays. In so doing, it emits a pair of particles. The particles are linked forever in this way: the laws of nature dictate that if one of the particles is spinning in a way that we can call clockwise, then the other particle is spinning counterclockwise.

Now, let's say that you measure the spin of one of the particles. It turns up clockwise. By this very act of measurement, then, you have *determined* the spin of the other particle— even if it is at the other end of the universe. Einstein called this "spooky action at the distance," but it has been proved right time and again. What happens, according to physicists' current interpretation, is that each particle exists in two states simultaneously, somehow spinning clockwise and counterclockwise at the same time. Only when an observer makes a measurement on one particle does that particle settle down and choose one spin. This choice affects which spin its partner chooses. This suggests to some scholars a level of reality beyond the familiar everyday one, a reality in which spatial distance is meaningless (because the second particle receives the information about the first particle's choice simultaneously and makes its own choice based on that instantaneously). It is in this other level of reality that some find a place for the existence of a supreme being.

A Restored Sense of Wonder

Twentieth-century discoveries in astronomy and cosmology—"the charts and the diagrams," to say nothing of the formulas and calculations—are not sending us "tired and sick," fleeing like Whitman back into the mysteries of "the moist night" to take refuge in our ignorance. Instead, astronomers' findings—both the new nebulae and novas and galaxies they spy with their telescopes and the inferences they draw about the orbs scattered across the universe—are restoring a sense of wonder, and even of purpose, in a world

74

at times hostile to both. Instead of leaving less and less room for a Creator who, at least once, acted in the world, they are acting as an inspiration to and support for faith.

This is a momentous switch. Science has been pilloried for centuries for robbing the world of its enigmatic beauty and for squeezing God out of the picture. Like kudzu creeping over the landscape of the South, it spread into the realm of religion until there was not a patch of territory that religion could claim as its own. Finally, science, the bogeyman of faith, is undergoing a radical change in its place in human culture. . . .

The discoveries that come streaming in from our telescopes are inspiring thoughtful people not to subsume science to faith or faith to science, but to seek an accommodation between the two. It is this quest that is winning adherents as the millennium begins. Science and religion illuminate different mysteries, all agree, casting their light on different questions. But each can heal the worst excesses of the other, with science, as Pope John Paul II said, "purify[ing] religion from error and superstition," and religion "purify[ing] science from idolatry and false absolutes" by infusing it with a little humility. Or, as Einstein observed, "Science without religion is lame, religion without science is blind."

Two Ways of Looking at the World

The new scholarship of science and theology suggests, too, that they have one thing in common: the motivation that animates both in the search for scientific truths and the search for spiritual meaning. "I think that fundamentally the impetus for the two quests is the same," says Carl Feit, a biologist and practicing Jew. "Religion and science are two ways of looking at the world, and each helps guide our search for understanding. Profoundly religious people are asking the same questions as profound scientists: Who are we? And what are we? What's the purpose? What's the end? Where do we come from? And where are we going? We have this need, this desire, this drive, to understand ourselves and the world that we live in."

When Václav Havel, the poet and president of the Czech Republic, received the Liberty Medal in Philadelphia on the

218th anniversary of the Declaration of Independence, he described the societal transition underway in the world. Science, he said, has become alienated from the lives we lead. For too long it has failed "to connect with the most intrinsic nature of reality and with natural human experience. It is now more a source of disintegration and doubt than a source of integration and meaning." But he saw a glimmer of hope. "Paradoxically, inspiration for the renewal of this lost integrity can once again be found in science . . . a science producing ideas that in a certain sense allow it to transcend its own limits. . . . Transcendence is the only real alternative to extinction," especially the extinction of the collective human soul. That was in 1994. Now, as the millennium turns, Havel's hope that science would cease to be a source of doubt and become a source of inspiration is becoming realized.

At the end of the 20th century, it is in what science is unearthing about nature that we are seeing confirmation of existing religious beliefs or inspiration for a whole new kind of faith. We are not fusing religion and science; the two will always retain their separate identities. But from scholars to churchgoers to those who have turned their backs on organized religion, we are seeking and finding today in the discoveries of science—and especially in the discoveries of astronomy and cosmology—what in eras past only religion has offered: solace and support. A sense of connection between the otherwise insignificant human mind and the tapestry of creation. A sense of wonder, and of awe; a sense that the world is rational; a sense, even, of the sacred. And, to believers, hints of the nature and character of God.

CHAPTER 3

How Do Religions
Give Life Meaning?

Chapter Preface

In her book *Amazing Grace*, writer Kathleen Norris discusses her return to the Christian church after many years away. Struggling with what she calls a "justifiable distrust of institutional religions,'" Norris's gradual conversion started with a recognition that her understanding of her parents' faith was incomplete and undeveloped. For a time she had thought she was free of religious "fetters," but she ultimately found that she could not dismiss her religious heritage: "In religious development, as in psychological development, we must become our own person. But denial of our inheritance doesn't work, nor does simply castigating it as 'nothing.'"

The world's religions are—like art, mythology, and history—part of humanity's inheritance. Whether or not one subscribes to religious belief, an examination of religion reveals some of humanity's greatest hopes, deepest fears, and most profound vulnerabilities. This chapter explores five major world religions as well as two alternative approaches to spirituality.

In the first selection, Louis Finkelstein explains that the central doctrine of Judaism is the belief in a unified, self-revealing God who made himself known to the prophet Moses at Mount Sinai. For Jews, life's meaning revolves around God's special covenant with Israel as revealed through Moses. Rabbis, those entrusted to teach the religious law, serve as authorities in clarifying this covenant.

Christianity is built upon the foundation of Judaism because Jesus, whom Christians believe to be the son of God, was a practicing Jew and a rabbi. The viewpoints by Donald E. Miller and Bob George examine two general tendencies in Christianity. Liberal Christians, according to Miller, often interpret the scriptures as symbolic documents and seek to apply Jesus's teachings to current social and political concerns. Conservative Christians, according to George, believe that the Bible is based on historical fact and that the scriptures are the source of authoritative truth about God. All Christians see Jesus as the savior of humankind, but liberals tend to emphasize the salvation of society while conservatives first seek the salvation of the individual.

Islam, like Christianity, is also rooted in Judaism. While Muslims accept the teachings of Moses and Jesus, they believe that God's purest and final revelation is the Koran, a sacred text revealed to the prophet Muhammad. According to Hazrat Mirza Ghulam Ahmad, the ultimate goal in life for a Muslim is a complete surrender to the one true God, Allah. This goal is achieved through a process of purification involving disciplined prayer, perseverance, and divine grace.

Two religions that developed in Asia and that have shaped the lives of large numbers of people are Hinduism and Buddhism. Sarvepalli Radhakrishnan explores the universality of Hinduism, which accepts all paths to God (Brahman), the ultimate "heart of reality." In Hinduism, he explains, it is understood that people are at different levels of their understanding of God, so the divine might express itself in an incarnation like Krishna, in an ancestor, or in a wooden idol— but all serve as paths to the same reality. Buddhism also seeks the ultimate reality, asserts Gill Farrer-Halls, but it does not profess faith in a creator God. Instead, Buddhists seek liberation from suffering through meditation, detachment from desire, and the cultivation of compassion. The teachings of the Buddha, like-minded friends, and other "enlightened ones" help guide the individual toward enlightenment.

Finally, Riane Eisler and Wayne Teasdale discuss nontraditional expressions of spirituality. Eisler maintains that we should reclaim the ancient Goddess tradition in order to reconnect with the feminine aspect of the divine. In doing so, she maintains, humans will build a truly egalitarian and ecologically sustainable society. Teasdale also believes that a just and peaceful civilization is possible. He contends that interfaith dialogue and interspirituality—an approach to faith that embraces the inner truths in all religions—can transform humanity.

A greater understanding of various belief systems invites us to contemplate the human search for meaning across the barriers of time, place, and culture. As such, a consideration of religion is essential to constructing a life philosophy.

"Judaism is a way of life that endeavors to transform virtually every human action into a means of communion with God."

Judaism Is a Life of Communing with God

Louis Finkelstein

Louis Finkelstein (1895–1991) served as a professor and as chancellor at the Jewish Theological Seminary of America. He was considered to be the dominant leader of Conservative Judaism in the twentieth century and was the author and editor of many scholarly works, including the two-volume work *The Jews: Their History, Culture, and Religion*, from which this viewpoint is excerpted. Finkelstein maintains that Judaism is a way of life in which people seek to commune with God in every area of their lives. The central doctrine of Judaism, he explains, is the belief in one God. The will of God is found in the Law, which was given to the prophet Moses on Mount Sinai. Ordained rabbis teach and clarify the Law with the help of thousands of years of oral and written interpretations.

As you read, consider the following questions:
1. According to the ceremonial Law, when and where should Jews pray?
2. What is the Talmud, according to Finkelstein?
3. According to the author, how do Reform, Orthodox, and Conservative Jews differ?

Louis Finkelstein, "The Jewish Religion: Its Beliefs and Practices," *The Jews: Their History, Culture, and Religion*, edited by Louis Finkelstein. New York: HarperCollins, 1960. Copyright © 1949, 1955, 1960 by Louis Finkelstein. Reproduced by permission.

Judaism is a way of life that endeavors to transform virtually every human action into a means of communion with God. Through this communion with God, the Jew is enabled to make his contribution to the establishment of the Kingdom of God and the brotherhood of men on earth. So far as its adherents are concerned, Judaism seeks to extend the concept of right and wrong to every aspect of their behavior. Jewish rules of conduct apply not merely to worship, ceremonial, and justice between man and man, but also to such matters as philanthropy, personal friendships and kindnesses, intellectual pursuits, artistic creation, courtesy, the preservation of health, and the care of diet.[1]

Jewish Law

So rigorous is this discipline, as ideally conceived in Jewish writings, that it may be compared to those specified for members of religious orders in other faiths. A casual conversation or a thoughtless remark may, for instance, be considered a grave violation of Jewish Law. It is forbidden, as a matter not merely of good form but of religious law, to use obscene language, to rouse a person to anger, or to display unusual ability in the presence of the handicapped. The ceremonial observances are equally detailed. The ceremonial Law expects each Jew to pray thrice every day, if possible at the synagogue; to recite a blessing before and after each meal; to thank God for any special pleasure, such as a curious sight, the perfume of a flower, or the receipt of good news; to wear a fringed garment about his body; to recite certain passages from Scripture each day; and to don *tephillin* (cubical receptacles containing certain biblical passages) during the morning prayers.

Decisions regarding right and wrong under given conditions are not left for the moment, but are formulated with great care in the vast literature created by the Jewish religious teachers. At the heart of this literature are the Hebrew

1. Without desiring to ascribe to them any responsibility for this statement, the author records with deep gratitude the assistance in its preparation given by colleagues from different schools of Jewish thought. These include Rabbis Max Arzt, Ben Zion Bokser, Samuel S. Cohon, Judah Goldin, Israel M. Goldman, Simon Greenberg, David de Sola Pool, Samuel Schulman, and Aaron J. Tofield.

Scriptures, usually described as the Old Testament, consisting of the Five Books of Moses (usually called the *Torah*), the Prophets and the Hagiographa. These works, particularly the Five Books of Moses, contain the prescriptions for human conduct composed under Divine inspiration. The ultimate purpose of Jewish religious study is the application of the principles enunciated in the Scriptures, to cases and circumstances the principles do not explicitly cover.

Because Judaism is a way of life, no confession of faith can by itself make one a Jew. Belief in the dogmas of Judaism must be expressed in the acceptance of its discipline rather than in the repetition of a verbal formula. But no failure either to accept the beliefs of Judaism or to follow its prescriptions is sufficient to exclude from the fold a member of the Jewish faith. According to Jewish tradition, the covenant between God and Moses on Mt. Sinai included all those who were present and also all their descendants. . . . There is therefore no need for any ceremony to admit a Jewish child into the faith of Judaism. Born in a Jewish household, he becomes at once "a child of the covenant." The fact that the child has Jewish parents involves the assumption of the obligations that God has placed on these parents and their descendants. . . .

Judaism and Government

Like other religions, Judaism can be, and indeed has been, practiced under various forms of civil government: monarchical, semi-monarchical, feudal, democratic, and totalitarian. Adherents of the Jewish faith, like those of other religions, regard themselves as citizens or subjects of their respective states. In every synagogue prayers are offered for the safety of the government of the country of its location; and in the ancient Temple of Jerusalem daily sacrifices were offered on behalf of the imperial Roman government, as long as Palestine remained under its dominion. This patriotic loyalty to the state has often persisted in the face of cruel persecution. The principle followed has been that formulated by the ancient teacher, Rabbi Haninah. "Pray for the welfare of the government; for without fear of the government, men would have swallowed each other up alive."

Despite this ability to adjust itself to the exigencies of any form of temporal government, Judaism, like other faiths derived from the Prophets, has always upheld the principles of the Fatherhood of God and the dignity and worth of man as the child and creature of God; and its ideals are more consistent with those of democracy than any other system of government.

The Transforming Power of the Spirit

Judaism . . . came into the world to protest the tight alignment of spirituality with oppression in the religious life of both Egypt and Babylonia/Assyria/Persia—and to testify to a very different conception of the spiritual than the one that prevailed among ancient imperial societies. On the basis of the slave rebellion recounted in Exodus, Judaism explicitly called for a redistribution of wealth and for a spiritual order that would restore the fundamental justice, equality, and dignity of each individual.

Equally important, Judaism proclaimed that "cruelty is not destiny," that the world could be radically transformed, and that what makes that possible is YHVH—the four letters that stand for the Divine as the Force of Healing and Transformation of the universe. Nothing in the world was fixed, because the fundamental creative force of the universe, the Creator of the universe, was the YHVH Force that guaranteed that the world could be transformed from oppression and cruelty to a world based on love and caring.

Michael Lerner, *Spirit Matters*, 2000.

The most vigorous and consistent effort to formulate the discipline of Judaism in terms of daily life was that made in ancient Palestine and Babylonia. The Palestinian schools devoted to this purpose were founded in the second or third century before the Common Era, and flourished in their original form for six centuries and in a somewhat altered form until the Crusades. The Babylonian schools were founded in the third century of the Common Era and ended the first and most significant phase of their activity about three hundred years later.[2]

2. Cf. Judah Goldin, "The Period of the Talmud (135 B.C.E.—1035 C.E.)," this work, Vol. I, Chap. 3, *passim*.

The rules of conduct worked out in the discussion of these academies form the substance of Jewish Law. In arriving at these precepts, the ancient teachers were guided by their desire to know the Will of God. So far as possible they sought to discover His will through an intensive study of the Scriptures. Where Scripture offered no clear guidance, they tried to ascertain His will by applying its general principles of moral right. In addition, they had a number of oral traditions, going back to antiquity, which they regarded as supplementary to the written Law, and equal to it in authority and inspiration.

The high purpose of the discussions made them of monumental importance to Judaism. As a result, they were committed to memory by eager and faithful disciples, until the memorized materials grew to such proportions that it had to be reduced to writing. The work in which the discussions were thus preserved is known as the Talmud. . . .

The Place of Study in Judaism

It is impossible to understand Judaism without an appreciation of the place it assigns to the study and practice of the talmudic Law. Doing the Will of God is the primary spiritual concern of the Jew. Therefore, to this day, he must devote considerable time not merely to the mastery of the content of the Talmud, but also to training in its method of reasoning. The study of the Bible and the Talmud is thus far more than a pleasing intellectual exercise, and is itself a means of communication with God. According to some teachers, this study is the highest form of such communion imaginable.[3]

Because the preservation of the Divine will regarding human conduct is basic to all civilization, none of the commandments is more important than that of studying and teaching the Law. The most sacred object in Judaism is the Scroll containing the Five Books of Moses. Every synagogue must contain at least one copy of it. The Scroll must be placed in a separate Ark, before which burns an eternal light. The position of this Ark in the synagogue is in the direction

3. Cf. the essay on "Study as a Mode of Worship," by Professor Nathan Isaacs, in *The Jewish Library*, edited by Rabbi Leo Jung, 1928, pp. 51–70.

of Jerusalem; everyone turns toward the Ark in prayer. When the Scroll is taken from the Ark for the purpose of reading, all those present must rise. No irreverent or profane action may be performed in a room which contains a Scroll, nor may a Scroll be moved from place to place except for the performance of religious rites. From time to time the Scroll must be examined to ascertain that its writing is intact. . . .

No less important than this homage paid to the Scroll as symbol of the Law, is that paid to the living Law itself. Fully three-fourths of the Hebrew literature produced within the first nineteen centuries of the Common Era, is devoted to the elucidation of the Law. Many of the best minds in Judaism have been devoted to its study. Every parent is required to teach his child its basic elements. Its study is considered vital not only for the guidance it offers in the practice of Judaism, but for liberation from the burden of secular ambition and anxieties. The study of the Law is believed to be a foretaste of the immortal life, for the Sages of the Talmud believed that Paradise itself could offer men no nearer communion with God than the opportunity of discovering His will in the study of the Law.

The Talmud derives its authority from the position held by the ancient academies. The teachers of those academies, both of Babylonia and of Palestine, were considered the rightful successors of the older Sanhedrin, or Supreme Court, which before the destruction of Jerusalem (in the year 70 of the Common Era) was the arbiter of Jewish Law and custom. The Sanhedrin derived its authority from the statement in Deut. 17:8–13, that whenever a question of interpretation of the Law arises, it is to be finally decided by the Sages and priests in Jerusalem.

The Role of Rabbis

At the present time, the Jewish people have no living central authority comparable in status to the ancient Sanhedrin or the later academies. Therefore any decision regarding the Jewish religion must be based on the Talmud, as the final resume of the teachings of those authorities when they existed. The right of an individual to decide questions of religious Law depends entirely on his knowledge of the Bible, the Talmud, and the later manuals based on them, and upon his fidelity to their teachings. Those who have acquired this knowledge are called rabbis. There is no sharp distinction in religious status between the rabbi and the layman in Judaism. The rabbi is simply a layman especially learned in Scripture and Talmud. Nor is there any hierarchical organization or government among the rabbis of the world. Yet some rabbis, by virtue of their special distinction in learning, by common consent come to be regarded as superior authorities on questions of Jewish Law. Difficult and complicated issues are referred to them for clarification.

Learning Is Sweet

In many traditional Jewish communities, when a child entered cheder, religious school, for the first time, that child was greeted by a curious sight: a chart of letters smeared with honey. The new student licked off the honey from the letters one by one, thus learning a critical lesson: learning is sweet, and the very letters of the word carry the sweetness.

David Wolpe, quoted in *Spiritual Literacy*, Frederic and Mary Ann Brussat, eds., 1996.

To be recognized as a rabbi, a talmudic student customarily is ordained. Traditionally, the authority to act as a rabbi may be conferred by any other rabbi. It is usual, however, for students at various theological schools to receive this authority from their teachers. In America, there are several rabbinical schools, each of which ordains its graduates in the manner in which degrees are conferred on graduates of other institutions of learning. . . . There is considerable variation among the interpretations of Judaism taught at these seminaries, and consequently there is a considerable difference in emphasis on the subjects included in their respective curricula. This has resulted from the fact that during the second half of the nineteenth century various groups of rabbis, primarily in Germany and America, claimed authority not merely to interpret but also to amend talmudic, and even biblical Law. These rabbis are known as Reform rabbis, and their congregations as Reform congregations. Of the rabbis who adhere to traditional Judaism, some reject any significant innovations from customary practice; these rabbis are called Orthodox. Others maintain that Jewish law is a living tradition, subject to change, but they insist that such changes must be made in accordance with traditional canons for the interpretation and development of Rabbinic law. These rabbis are usually called Conservative.[4]

The difference between the various groups of American rabbis have not led to any sectarian schism. Although the difference in practice between the traditional and Reform groups is considerable, each accepts the other as being within the fold of Judaism. It is possible for them to do so, because of the principle that even an unobservant or a heretical Jew does not cease to be a member of the covenant made between God and Israel at the time of the Revelation. Only actual rejection of Judaism, by affiliation with another faith, is recognized as separating one from the Jewish community. So long as a follower of the Jewish faith has not by overt act or word and of his own free will declared himself a member of another religion, other Jews are bound to regard him as one of their own faith, and to seek his return to its practice and beliefs. . . .

The Basic Concepts of Judaism

The central doctrine of Judaism is the belief in the One God, the Father of all mankind. The first Hebrew words a Jewish child learns are the confession of faith contained in the verse "Hear, O Israel, the Lord is our God, the Lord is One," and every believing Jew hopes that as he approaches his end in the fullness of time he will be sufficiently conscious to repeat this same confession. This monotheistic belief is subject to no qualification or compromise. . . .

There is a wide variety of interpretation among Rabbinical scholars, both ancient and modern, with regard to the concepts of Judaism. In some instances, the differences of interpretation are so great that it is difficult to speak of a concept as being basically or universally Jewish or Rabbinic.

4. For a survey of the Orthodox, Conservative, and Reform movements in the United States, see Moshe Davis, *Jewish Religious Life and Institutions in America (A Historical Study)*, pp. 310f., 326f.

There are thus a number of concepts, each having its own limited authority and following.

This applies also to a degree to the fundamental beliefs which have been brought together in the best known Jewish creed, that of Maimonides. According to this creed, there are thirteen basic dogmas in Judaism. They are as follows:

1. The belief in God's existence.
2. The belief in His unity.
3. The belief in His incorporeality.
4. The belief in His timelessness.
5. The belief that He is approachable through prayer.
6. The belief in prophecy.
7. The belief in the superiority of Moses to all other prophets.
8. The belief in the revelation of the Law, and that the Law as contained in the Pentateuch is that revealed to Moses.
9. The belief in the immutability of the Law.
10. The belief in Divine providence.
11. The belief in Divine justice.
12. The belief in the coming of the Messiah.
13. The belief in the resurrection and human immortality.

| "*Although Scripture and tradition are important, the basepoint of liberal morality has been reason.*"

Liberal Christianity Combines Reason with Faith

Donald E. Miller

Donald E. Miller teaches in the School of Religion at the University of Southern California, where he specializes in the sociology of religion and the relationship between ethical analysis and the social sciences. In the following viewpoint Miller defines liberal Christianity as an evolving belief system that values art, science, culture, and social justice in addition to the teachings of Jesus and the prophets of the Old Testament. In contrast to conservative Christians, liberal Christians often interpret the Scriptures as symbolic documents rather than historically accurate accounts, Miller points out. Believing that God cannot be fully defined by the limited human mind, liberal Christians approach God as the ultimate meaning and ground of being.

As you read, consider the following questions:
1. According to Miller, what interpretive principle do liberal Christians apply when reading the Bible?
2. How do liberal and conservative Christians differ in their view of humanity's relationship with God, according to the author?
3. What is symbolic realism, according to Miller?

Donald E. Miller, *The Case for Liberal Christianity*. San Francisco, CA: Harper & Row Publishers, 1981. Copyright © 1981 by Donald E. Miller. Reproduced by permission of HarperCollins Publishers.

One of the central facts of contemporary existence is the diversity of meaning systems that individuals follow. Liberal Christianity is one framework of meaning and values. In addition to being unique as a religious framework of meaning—as opposed to a strictly secular framework, which makes no reference to things sacred, or to a transcendent reference point for evaluating the meaningfulness of human existence—liberal Christianity is distinctive insofar as it is one of several perspectives within the Christian religious framework. . . .

Defining Liberal Christianity

Liberal Christians differ from their more conservative counterparts at a number of points, but let me begin with their *view toward culture*. Rather than perceiving culture, particularly science and the arts, as a potential threat to religious faith, liberal Christians have understood that Christianity must evolve and adapt itself—or at least its expression—from age to age. They have believed that the application of the gospel must be reinterpreted from each new cultural context. Although there may be a core essence to Christianity, liberal Christians view accommodation to culture as necessary and positive, if what one means by "accommodation" is that they should seek to understand God and their moral responsibility in terms of the best available scientific knowledge and social analysis.

The Arts and Education

Liberal Christians look upon the arts as important expressions of the problems and tensions of their culture. Liberal Christians also recognize the invaluable moral critiques found in many artistic expressions. Whereas film, theater, and dance may be shunned by many conservative Christians, liberal Christians look to these artistic productions as important occasions for not only self-reflection, but also a potential uplifting and enlivening of the human spirit. Liberal Christians have long recognized that things ultimate and real can be portrayed through a variety of mediums. Thus, an evening spent reading a novel, viewing a theatrical production, or seeing a movie may be as illuminating as a comparable period of time spent reading the Bible. Liberal Christians believe that revelations may come in many forms.

Liberals have long been champions of education. They find that nothing is to be feared in knowledge. To discover the relativity of cultures is not a new insight so much as it is a foundation stone on which liberalism rests. Liberal clergy have usually been highly educated. The task implicit in sermon preparation by liberal clergy has been to blend creatively the "old gospel" with the personal, social, and political problems felt by those in the pew. As a result, psychological, sociological, and philosophical insights often have found their way into the text of sermons given by the liberal clergy. Book discussion groups have been at least as common in liberal churches as Bible study groups and prayer meetings.

The danger in liberalism is that the Christian message may become a mirror reflection of the spirit of the age. This is an ever-present problem for liberal Christians to confront. On the other hand, liberals have protested that one cannot possibly critique culture without understanding it. . . .

Morality

Liberal Christians have always placed considerable emphasis upon the moral witness of their faith. Rooted in the Social Gospel Movement of the last several decades of the nineteenth century and the first three decades of the twentieth century, liberal Christianity has always sought to apply its Gospel to the social betterment of the human community. Political rallies and social action committee meetings have often taken the place of more traditionally pious activities. In its earlier period, liberalism was married to the spirit of socialism. As political winds changed, so did the social ethic of liberal Christianity. Under the pressure of the Neo-orthodox Movement, many liberals were forced into a greater acknowledgment of the reality of sin and of the necessity of a newfound political realism. Whatever the ideology, however, liberal Christians have always found themselves in the streets, politicking city councils, writing letters to congressmen, and busying themselves with social welfare concerns. Their approach stands in contrast to that of many conservative Christians who have sought to change the world by changing hearts (through conversion).

Although Scripture and tradition are important, the base-point of liberal morality has been reason. This emphasis, of course, has coincided nicely with the commitment of liberal Christians to education. In contrast to the scriptural "proof-texting" of many conservative Christians, liberals have often appealed to the broader principles of justice and love as explicated in the Bible. Reason has always been the mediating force in applying these biblical insights to particular situations. Not infrequently liberals have endorsed a contextual or situational ethic. They have been relatively inhospitable, on the other hand, to moral legalisms. Always reason is to be used in weighing the authority of Scripture and tradition. . . .

Another identifying mark of the moral commitment of liberal Christians is that they have characteristically given at least as much attention to social morality as personal morality. Matters of sexual practice and personal vice have been of interest to liberal Christians, but programmatic emphases have more typically been related to issues of war, poverty, racial discrimination, employment practices, and so forth. Systemic and social-structural problems have been understood to be at the root of much of the suffering and misery in the world. For this reason, the prophets of the Old Testament have often been appealed to as frequently as the teachings of Jesus.

Scripture

Liberal Christians differ from conservative Christians in that they generally approach Scripture nondogmatically. Liberal biblical scholars tend to apply historical, sociological, and even psychological tools and insights to their interpretations of Scripture. The hermeneutical principle often applied is that everything—Scripture included—is written within a cultural context. Therefore, to understand the meaning of a document, one must understand how and why it was written. One must also understand the worldview of the writer. For example, one of the most famous biblical scholars, Rudolf Bultmann, believed that the New Testament was written from the perspective of a prescientific cosmology of a three-tiered universe (with heaven above, hell or the underworld below, and the earth, on which men and women dwell, as a

mediating structure between the two). His task of demythol-
ogization was an effort to get at the kerygma (message)
which lay behind this first century worldview.

The Bible Is Not God

The Bible is not God. It is a collection of stories and teachings told by an ancient people concerning their experience
with God. Sometimes they were wrong, and sometimes they
were right on the money. This point of view will make some
nervous ("Well, if we can pick and choose what to believe,
what good is it?"). But it will also return ultimate truth to
where it belongs: to God. God will highlight and burn in our
souls from scripture what we need to hear and heed. God will
use this imperfect, human document (what other kind of material does God have to work with in this human life, anyway?)
to awaken us to the miracle of our life. God will use teachers,
friends, books, and the Spirit within to sort out what is eternally true from what is culturally misguided in scripture.

On the other hand, as people of the biblical tradition, we
take the Bible seriously. For we recognize that it represents
centuries of broad experience, an experience of thousands of
people, many of whom were utterly devoted to and graced by
God in profound ways. This representation far outweighs
the limited experience of our own individual lives. While we
may have more wisdom than one or another of the particular voices of scripture, we cannot make this claim about the
broad themes and recurring truths that shine through its human limitations.

Brian C. Taylor, *Setting the Gospel Free*, 1996.

When the Scriptures are understood as human documents, they then are susceptible to all the canons of modern
historical and literary analysis. To the liberal theologian,
there is a considerable difference between viewing the Bible
primarily through the eyes of faith and being equally open to
a cultural and historical perspective. Historically, the resurrection of Jesus and the virgin birth are at best ambiguous as
concrete occurrences. From the perspective of faith, however, they may have quite a different significance. But one
should never conclude that the Scriptures are unimportant
for the liberal Christian. Quite the contrary, they are central
to the Christian faith. The fact that more attention is given

93

to them as symbolic documents than as historical documents does not distort their importance.

After all, liberal Christianity (as well as fundamentalist Christianity) is based upon a message whose inspiration is taken from the life and teachings of Jesus. Whatever accommodations are to be made in applying Christianity to the contemporary setting, the liberal Christian is nevertheless compelled to go back to the rather radical teachings of Jesus concerning the kingdom. Any compromises to be made with the Sermon on the Mount, for example, are self-consciously made by understanding the setting in which Jesus was teaching and living. Likewise, any alterations of Paul's teachings on women are made, again, from the basis of an interpretation of Paul's social setting. Liberal Christians, by their very approach to Scripture, are spared the agony experienced by many conservatives who are forced, when they disagree with some biblical dictum on the grounds of social conscience, to go through what has been aptly described as a sort of "hermeneutical ventriloquism."

Man and God

A basic distinction to be drawn between liberal and conservative Christians concerns the issue of God's self-declaration to man. Most conservative Christians begin with the assumption that man exists as the creation of God, a supernatural being who is personal and therefore interested in communicating with his creation. Following on this assumption, conservative Christians postulate that God has revealed himself in time and space at a number of historical junctures, the most important being his decision to give earthly form to his son, Jesus. Jesus, then, is viewed as God's clearest self-declaration of who he is. Furthermore, conservative Christians postulate that God safeguarded his self-declaration by inspiring the writers of the Bible, giving them the very words to say (or, some would argue, only the thoughts were given—while others more liberal, but still within the conservative camp, would argue that God gave official sanction to what was penned by the biblical writers).

Liberal Christians, on the other hand, tend to see the above progression as much too anthropomorphic. Even the father-son imagery seems like a projection. Rather than starting with God, postulating divine initiative, many liberal Christians begin with the human predicament and emphasize *man's search* for God. According to this approach, from the standpoint of a functional definition, God is synonymous with the search for human wholeness, for confidence in the ultimate meaningfulness of human existence. Paul Tillich's definition of faith as the *state* of Ultimate Concern is representative of the liberal perspective because the emphasis is placed upon man's search for God.

Tillich's definition of God, too, is representative of the liberal position. God is the "God above God"—meaning that man's finite limitations forever leave man short of defining in any absolute way who God is. Nevertheless, to the extent that one dares to venture a definition, it is an expansive one: God is the very "Ground of Being"; God is "Being-Itself." These definitions are nonreductive. If liberals have a central objection to the view many conservative Christians pose of God, it is that the conservative view reduces God to understandable, human terms—or human projections. Tillich's view of God as the "Ground of Being" is in reaction to that first century cosmological perspective which put God up in the sky, sitting on a throne, looking down on his creation.

Liberal Christians have viewed God in a much more immanentistic fashion. God is within creation. He is the life-force. He is at the center of all change, all innovation, all creativity. He is the source of life and is experienced in those profound moments of joy, communion, celebration. God is the "Thou" of the I-Thou encounter. He is the Ground of Being. God is present in all those activities which unite people rather than divide them, which call upon persons to transcend self-interest through brotherhood and sisterhood. God is personal as we discover our own humanity and act in his name to realize community: that state in which we relate to others as "ends" and not "means" to self-centered purposes.

The finer expressions about God in the liberal tradition have not, however, made God totally immanent. While many liberal Christians may have moved toward a healthy mysticism in both their experience and their speech about God, they have maintained the tension between God as transcendant and God as immanent. In other words, they have recognized, above all, that it is idolatrous to reduce God to human standards. He is present within his creation, he is the source of all meaning, he is at the center of all ethical structures, and yet he stands above and outside that which is purely human as the judge of all human projects. He is the "I am" of the Old Testament. He is one to both fear and worship. . . .

Symbolic Realism

Sociologist Robert Bellah has identified an important distinction between two types of "realism" that separate conservatives from liberals. Conservatives tend to be "historical realists" to the extent that they believe the truth of Christianity is found in the historical acts witnessed to in the New Testament—such as literal miracles, a literal bodily resurrection, and so forth. Historical realists are interested in understanding history "as it was." They take a nonmetaphorical and nonfigurative approach to interpreting Scripture. . . . Hence, one is "saved" if one believes that the Bible is the inspired word of God, that Jesus is the literal son of God sent down to earth to atone for mankind's sins, that he died on the cross and three days later was miraculously raised from the dead, and that he presently lives with God, sitting at his right hand.

The liberal "symbolic realists," in contrast, emphasize that "meaning" is always a product of the interaction between subject and object. Meaning is *granted* to events—it is not considered inherent in them. According to this view, the Scriptures contain the record of men's and women's reflections regarding the *meaning* which Christ had *for them*. It is not primarily an historical account. The resurrection, the miracles, the virgin birth are valued as symbols that point beyond the historical event to a larger and more ultimate truth. But the truth does not lie in the symbols (as historical events). Symbols are irreducible. They are not identical with actual events, although they may derive from them. To take symbols literally is to engage in idolatry. Symbolic realists have given up hope of discovering what "really happened"; indeed, most of them are not even convinced that such knowledge would make much difference.

The symbols that surround the life of Christ—parables, stories, sayings, etc.—are understood by liberal Christians to be vitally important. It is through the symbol of Christ (which is a complex symbol, indeed) that men and women may come to know God. The symbolic form of Christ, as presented in the Gospel accounts, however, points beyond any purely historical events to a transcendent Truth or Reality (which we symbolize as God)—this is the hope and faith of liberal Christians. . . .

The Need for Christian Liberalism

It is my opinion that what is needed in the churches today is a widescale recovery of the liberal spirit. . . .

Our social situation is ripe for a rebirth of Christian liberalism. But the ethical perspective of liberalism is only one reason for the return. Even more persuasive, in my view, is the fact that Christendom has become polarized. With a burgeoning population of evangelicals on one side and radical secularists on the other, the *mediating position, I would say, the temperate alternative*—of liberalism is being lost. Many young people today are unaware that there even is an option to the left of evangelicalism. And for many secularists, particularly young people, the only alternative to evangelicalism—if one wants to be religious—is membership with the "Moonies" or the Hare Krishna cult. . . .

In my view, liberalism is the most viable mode for reasserting the value of the Christian perspective to contemporary culture.

"Only through the Scriptures can we learn absolute, authoritative truth about God, man, salvation, and life."

Conservative Christianity Is a Biblical Relationship with God

Bob George

The Bible is the only source of truth about Jesus Christ and God, writes Bob George in the following viewpoint. Christianity is rooted in historical truth because the Bible presents objective, concrete facts—not fanciful tales or mythical legends, George contends. He claims that conservative Christians enter into a personal relationship with God's only son, Jesus, who gives gifts of wisdom to those who are humble and who recognize that they cannot rely solely on their intellect to understand scriptural truth. George has written several books that seek to make traditional Christianity more understandable to wide audiences. He is the head of a counseling organization as well as a radio talk-show host who advises people who call in.

As you read, consider the following questions:
1. In George's opinion, what makes Christianity unique in comparison with other religions?
2. What happens when people seek spiritual knowledge apart from the Scriptures, in the author's view?
3. According to George, what attributes do Christians need in order to grow in grace?

Bob George, *Growing in Grace*. Eugene, OR: Harvest House Publishers, 1997.
Copyright © 1997 by Harvest House Publishers. Reproduced by permission.

Christianity stands alone, separate from the world's religions, because of its unique combination of the astounding claims of the man Jesus of Nazareth and its pinpointing of those claims at a concrete place and time in history. For example, there have been many other religious teachers in history, such as Confucius, Buddha, and Muhammad, but none of these (nor any other man) ever claimed to be God and also convinced a significant number of followers that he actually was God.

Though people throughout the ages have believed in many different gods, these were known only through vague legends and myths. No one claimed to have personally known Zeus or Thor, for example. In the world's religions you either find a historical religious teacher who claimed to know a way to successful living but was a normal man nonetheless, or else you find fanciful stories of gods and other supernatural beings who lived no one knows where or when.

The Bible and History

However, when you turn to the Bible you find a relentless presentation of objective, historical facts. Persons, places, and times are concrete. Caesar Augustus, "while Quirinius was governor of Syria" (Luke 2:2),[1] ordered a census of the empire, "so Joseph also went up from the town of Nazareth in Galilee to Judea, to Bethlehem" (Luke 2:4). John the Baptist, the forerunner of Christ, began his ministry "in the fifteenth year of the reign of Tiberius Caesar" (Luke 3:1). Within a few weeks after Jesus' crucifixion, Peter was proclaiming in that very city of Jerusalem, "God has raised this Jesus to life, and *we are all witnesses of the fact*" (Acts 2:32). Throughout the following decades we see the message of Christ spreading like wildfire, fanned by the conviction that "we cannot help speaking about *what we have seen and heard*" (Acts 4:20). The most violent persecutor of Christians, Saul of Tarsus, is converted and later explains, "He appeared *to me* also" (1 Corinthians 15:7). With lightning speed, especially considering that this was a day without television, radio, or printing press, Christians are found throughout the

---

1. All biblical references are taken from the New International Version of the Bible.

Roman Empire. When the last remaining eyewitness writes his account he closes with "This is the disciple who testifies to these things and who wrote them down" (John 21:24).

Right in the middle of all this solid historical setting, as the cause and center of it all, is a man who claimed to be God!

Who Wrote the Bible?

From the human standpoint the Bible was written by not less than thirty-six authors over a period of about sixteen hundred years. But the important thing to remember is that these men wrote under the direct control of God. God guided them in writing the very words. This is what we mean by inspiration. The following Scriptures clearly teach that the Bible is inspired by God:

"For the prophecy came not in old time by the will of man, but holy men of God spake as they were moved by the Holy Ghost" (2 Peter 1:21).

"All Scripture is given by inspiration of God and is profitable for doctrine, for reproof, for correction, for instruction in righteousness; that the man of God may be perfect, thoroughly furnished unto all good works" (2 Timothy 3:16–17).

Thus the Bible *is* the word of God. It is not enough to say that the Bible *contains* the word of God. This might imply that parts of it are inspired and parts are not. *Every part of the Bible is inspired.* "All Scripture is given by inspiration of God."

Emmaus Bible College, *What Christians Believe*, 1949.

These things are not the result of blind faith or some emotional leap. They are presented as facts that are either true or are not. For almost 20 centuries, millions of men and women have examined these claims, have come to the conclusion that Jesus Christ is indeed alive and that He is Lord, and have entered into a personal relationship with Him. This is the foundation of our faith. It is rational, intelligent, and open to investigation. This brings me back to my main point: If we want to discover the real meaning and experience of "Christ in you," we must learn to take this same objective, clear-thinking faith that forms the foundation of Christianity and bring it into our daily lives. *Only in this way will we ever grow in grace.* The Jesus who made those claims almost 2000 years ago is now glorified and exalted at the Father's right hand, and He is the same living Christ who lives in and through us today through the indwelling Holy Spirit.

During His earthly ministry Jesus Christ continually pointed people to the Scriptures, the *written* Word that testified about Him, the *living* Word. In His criticism of the Pharisees He said, "If you believed Moses, you would believe Me, for he wrote about Me" (John 5:46). When He walked with the two disciples on the way to Emmaus after His resurrection, He challenged their despondent attitudes and said that it resulted from their unbelief.

> He said to them, "How foolish you are, and how slow of heart to believe all that the prophets have spoken! Did not the Christ have to suffer these things and then enter his glory?" And beginning with Moses and all the Prophets, He explained to them what was said in all the Scriptures *concerning Himself* (Luke 24.25–27).

Later, after appearing to His disciples in His resurrected form, He said to them:

> "This is what I told you while I was still with you: Everything must be fulfilled that is *written about Me* in the Law of Moses, the Prophets and the Psalms." Then He opened their minds so they could understand the Scriptures (Luke 24:44,45).

True Understanding of the Bible

It was necessary for Christ to open their minds, and to show them that the Scriptures, like history, are "His story." Today, He must open *our* minds before we can correctly understand the *meaning* of God's Word. First Corinthians 2:14 tells us, "The man without the Spirit does not accept the things that come from the Spirit of God, for they are foolishness to him, and he cannot understand them, because they are spiritually discerned." A true knowledge of Christ and His Word does not come through human intelligence, intellectual ability, or mere study. God says, "No eye has seen, no ear has heard, no mind has conceived what God has prepared for those who love Him" (1 Corinthians 2:9). How then can we discover the true knowledge of Christ? "God has revealed it to us by His Spirit" (1 Corinthians 2:10). That is exactly why you find so often in Paul's letters passages like this:

> For this reason, ever since I heard about your faith in the Lord Jesus and your love for all the saints, I have not stopped

giving thanks for you, remembering you in my prayers. I keep asking that the God of our Lord Jesus Christ, the glorious Father, *may give you the Spirit of wisdom and revelation, so that you may know Him better.* I pray also that *the eyes of your heart may be enlightened* in order that you may know the hope to which He has called you, the riches of His glorious inheritance in the saints, and His incomparably great power for us who believe (Ephesians 1:15–19).

Notice that wisdom and revelation are gifts from God, not learned attributes. Who does God give these gifts to? "God opposes the proud, but *gives grace to the humble*" (James 4:6). Recognition of who *Christ* is—God—and who *we* are—God's creation—demands a response of dependency from any intelligent, thinking person. However, our dependency on Christ is something of a paradox. On one hand, we need the written Word as our objective standard of truth; but on the other hand, we must live in dependence upon the Spirit of God to open our minds to a spiritual understanding beyond knowing mere words of ink on paper. God does not reveal truth *contrary to* His written Word, but neither does He want His people to become experts in His written Word whose goal is not to know the Person of Christ who is the living Word!

If we fall into the first error, that of seeking spiritual knowledge apart from the objective truth of the Scriptures, we are left defenseless and open to all kinds of mystical nonsense and error. We will find ourselves "tossed back and forth by the waves, and blown here and there by every wind of teaching and by the cunning and craftiness of men in their deceitful scheming" (Ephesians 4:14). Several times a week I receive calls on our radio program, "People to People," from listeners in this category. It is amazing to see the kinds of error that people can fall into who have no standard or plumbline of truth!. . .

In order to worship the *true* Christ, we must be worshiping the *biblical* Christ! Any other Jesus is a figment of man's imagination, which can neither save you nor enable you to walk in the newness of His life. To "believe in" a nonbiblical Jesus is really just a form of idolatry—man's tendency to worship a god of his own creation. Only through the Scriptures can we learn absolute, authoritative truth about God, man, salvation, and life.

But we can get off on the other side just as easily. Mere words printed on a page, knowledge of doctrines, or systematic theologies cannot satisfy the "God-shaped vacuum" in our hearts that cries out for a personal encounter with the living God. Sincere, dedicated Christians can still fall into the same error as the Pharisees, to whom Jesus said:

> You diligently study the Scriptures because you think that by them you possess eternal life. *These are the Scriptures that testify about Me, yet you refuse to come to Me* to have life (John 5:39, 40). . . .

All of God's truth is addressed to the humble—to people who recognize their need for grace, that they cannot understand truth on their own, that they cannot live the Christian life on their own. Proud people cannot receive grace because they *will not* receive grace. They are convinced of their own sufficiency and enamored by their own ability. Therefore they can learn the words and debate the Scriptures but still miss Christ. You can very easily have a highly trained intellect but a cold heart. . . .

In order to grow in grace we need both of these attitudes: a commitment to the Scriptures as God's revelation of truth for our lives, and a humble recognition of our dependency on the Spirit of God to empower us to know the God *of* the Scriptures.

> "The real object of man's life [is] . . . a true knowledge and worship of God and a total resignation to His will so that whatever is said or done is for His sake only."

Islam Entails a Submission to God's Will

Hazrat Mirza Ghulam Ahmad

Hazrat Mirza Ghulam Ahmad (1835–1908) was a *mujaddid*, a reformer and defender of Islam, who wrote numerous books to promote the Islamic faith. While living in British colonial India, he was a leader who taught that Islam was superior to Hinduism and Christianity. Later in his life, Ahmad worked to foster a greater respect for Islam in Europe. This viewpoint discusses the three levels of spiritual development available to all humans. To become moral beings, individuals must abandon their animal passions and undergo a purification process that ultimately leads to their complete submission and obedience to Allah, the one true God. Ahmad concludes by listing eight ways to attain this highest state of life.

As you read, consider the following questions:

1. What is the source of the "moral life" in humans, according to Ahmad?
2. According to the author, does the transformation of the soul occur during life or after death?
3. What are the eight ways to reach the goal of total submission to God, in Ahmad's view?

Hazrat Mirza Ghulam Ahmad, *Teachings of Islam*, translated by Maulana Muhammad Alie. Lanore, Pakistan: Ahmadiyyah Anjuman Isha'at Islam, 1910.

In the name of Allāh, the Beneficent, the Merciful—1:1. . . .

The first question relates to the physical, moral and spiritual conditions of man. The Quran observes this division by fixing three respective sources for this threefold condition of man, that is, three springs out of which these three conditions flow. The first of these in which the physical conditions of man take their birth is termed the *nafs al-ammāra*, which signifies the "uncontrollable spirit", or the "spirit prone to evil". . . .

It is characteristic of the *nafs al-ammāra* that it inclines man to evil, tends to lead him into iniquitous and immoral paths, and stands in the way of his attainment of perfection and moral excellence. Man's nature is prone to evil and transgression at a certain stage in his development, and so long as he is devoid of high moral qualities, this evil nature is predominant in him. He is subject to this state so long as he does not walk in the light of true wisdom and knowledge, but acts in obedience to the natural inclinations of eating, drinking, sleeping, becoming angry or excited, just like the lower animals.

As soon, however, as he frees himself from the control of animal passions and, guided by reason and knowledge, he holds the reins of his natural desires and governs them instead of being governed by them—when a transformation is worked in his soul from grossness to virtue—he then passes out of the physical state and is a moral being in the strict sense of the word.

The Self-Accusing Soul

The source of the moral conditions of man is called, in the terminology of the Quran, the *nafs al-lawwāma*, or the "self-accusing soul". . . .

This is the spring from which flows a highly moral life and, on reaching this stage, man is freed from bestiality. The swearing by the self-accusing soul indicates the regard in which it is held. For, the change from the disobedient to the self-accusing soul being a sure sign of its improvement and purification makes it deserving of approbation in the sight of the Almighty.

Lawwāma literally means "one who reproves severely", and the *nafs al-lawwāma* (self-accusing soul) has been so

105

called because it upbraids a man for the doing of evil deeds and strongly hates unbridled passions and bestial appetites. Its tendency, on the other hand, is to generate noble qualities and a virtuous disposition, to transform life so as to bring the whole course and conduct of it to moderation, and to restrain the carnal passions and sensual desires so as to keep them within due bound.

Although, as stated above, the "self-accusing soul" upbraids itself for its faults and frailties, yet it is not the master of its passions, nor is it powerful enough to practise virtue exclusively. The weakness of the flesh has the upper hand sometimes, and then it stumbles and falls down. Its weakness then resembles that of a child who does not wish to fall but whose legs are sometimes unable to support him. It does not, however, persist in its fault, every failure bringing a fresh reproach. At this stage, the soul is anxious to attain moral excellence, and revolts against disobedience which is the characteristic of the first, or the animal stage, but does, notwithstanding its yearning for virtue, sometimes deviate from the line of duty.

The Soul at Rest

The third or the last stage in the onward movement of the soul is reached on attaining to the source of all spiritual qualities. The soul at this stage is, in the words of the Quran, the *nafs al-mutma'inna*, or the "soul at rest". . . .

The soul is now freed from all weaknesses and frailties and is braced with spiritual strength. It is perfectly united with God and cannot live without Him. As water flows with great force down a slope and, on account of its great mass and the total absence of all obstacles, dashes down with irresistible force, so does the soul at this stage, casting off all trammels, flow unrestrained towards its Maker.

It is further clear from the words "O soul that art at rest with thy Lord, return to Him" that it is in this life, and not after death, that this great transformation is worked and that it is in this world, and not elsewhere, that access to paradise is granted to it. Again, as the soul has been commanded to return to its Master, it is clear that such a soul finds its support only in its Supporter. The love of God is its food, and

The Five Pillars of Islam

There are five pillars to Islam. The first pillar is the Muslims' ultimate profession of their faith, the *shadada: la ilaha illa Allah; Muhammad rasul Allah*, "There is no god but Allah, and Muhammad is the prophet of Allah." . . .

The second pillar . . . is prayer (*salaat*), which is carried out five times a day: at dawn, noon, mid-afternoon, sunset, and after the fall of darkness or at bedtime. The actual prayers are accompanied by ritual cleansing, hand gestures, body bows and prostrations. . . .

The third pillar . . . involves a serious redistribution of wealth. Since all is given by God, then nothing of what I own is mine, unless it is shared according to God's will. . . . The intent [is] . . . to give to the poor and to be a just and peace-filled society. . . .

The fourth pillar . . . is the fast that takes place during the holy month of Ramadan, the ninth month of the Muslim calendar. . . . All Muslims all over the world during Ramadan are called on to fast for thirty days, unless they are sick or on a journey. The aim of abstaining from food during the day is to help Muslims identify with the poor, who cannot choose when, where and what to eat. . . .

The fifth pillar of Islam . . . is the pilgrimage (*hajj*) to Mecca. This obligation does what all great pilgrimages do: it restarts the conversion experience by returning the devotee to the point of origin.

Meg Funk, *Islam Is* . . . , 2003.

---

it drinks deep at this fountain of life and is, therefore, delivered from death. . . .

The Goal of Life

The real object of man's life according to the Quran is, therefore, a true knowledge and worship of God and a total resignation to His will so that whatever is said or done is for His sake only. One thing, at least, is plain: man has no choice in the matter of fixing the aim of life. He is a creature, and the Creator, Who has brought him into existence and bestowed upon him higher and more excellent faculties than upon other animals, has also assigned an object to his existence. A man may or may not understand it, or a hundred different motives may hold him back from it, but the truth is that the grand aim of man's life consists in knowing and worshiping God and living for His sake. . . .

We are now in a position to answer the second part of the question: how can this object possibly be attained?

The **first** means towards the attainment of this end is that, in the recognition of the Lord, a man should tread upon the right path and have his faith in the true and living God. The goal can never be reached by the man who takes the first step in the wrong direction and looks upon some stone or creature or an element of nature as his deity. The true Master assists those who seek Him, but a dead deity cannot assist its dead worshippers. . . .

The **second** means to attain the true object of life consists in being informed of the perfect beauty which the Benefactor possesses. Beauty naturally attracts the heart and incites love. The beauty of God consists in His unity, His majesty, His grandeur and His other lofty attributes. . . .

The **third** means of reaching the goal consists in realizing the immense goodness of the Lord. . . .

The **fourth** means for the desired end is prayer. . . .

The **fifth** means is to seek God by spending one's substance and faculties, and sacrificing one's life and applying one's wisdom in His way:

> And strive hard in Allah's way with your wealth and your lives . . .—9:41. . . .

The **sixth** means by which a person may safely attain to the goal is perseverance, that is, he should be indefatigable in the way in which he walks and unswerving under the hardest trial:

> (As for) those who say, Our Lord is Allah, then continue in the right way, the angels descend upon them, saying: Fear not, nor be grieved, and receive good news of the Garden which you were promised. We are your friends in this world's life and in the Hereafter . . .—41:30–31.

In these verses, we are told that perseverance in faith brings about the pleasure of God. It is true, as the Arabic proverb goes, that "perseverance is more than a miracle." The highest degree of perseverance is called forth when adversities encompass a man all around, when he is threatened with loss of life, property and honour in the Divine path. . . .

The **seventh** means to attain the object is to keep company with the righteous and to imitate their perfect example. . . .

The **eighth** means is true visions and revelations from God. As the path which leads to the Creator is a secret and mysterious one, and is full of difficulties and dangers, the spiritual wayfarer may depart from the right course or despair of attaining the goal. The Divine grace, therefore, continues to encourage and strengthen him in his spiritual journey, gives him consolation in moments of grief and animates him with a still more zealous desire to pursue his journey eagerly.

Such is the Divine law with the wayfarers of His path that He continues to cheer their hearts with His word and to reveal to them that He is with them! Thus strengthened, they undertake this journey with great vigour. The Holy Book says:

> For them (the believers) is good news in this world's life and in the Hereafter.—10:64

It may be added that the Quran has described numerous other ways which assist us in reaching the goal of life, but we cannot describe them here for want of space.

*"When the Hindu found that different
people aimed at and achieved God-
realization in different ways, he generously
recognized them all and justified their
place in the course of history."*

Hinduism Teaches That All Ways Lead to God

Sarvepalli Radhakrishnan

Sarvepalli Radhakrishnan (1888–1975) is well known for introducing the thinking of Western philosophers into Indian thought and for introducing Indian philosophy to the Western world. He taught religion and ethics at Oxford University, served as an ambassador, and became the first vice-president and the second president of India. In the following viewpoint Radhakrishnan stresses the universality of Hinduism: its broad acceptance of all approaches to God. Hindus believe that humans see God in different ways and that the search for God comprises various stages and levels, but that all paths lead to the same ultimate reality, the author explains. In addition, Hinduism focuses on ethical conduct and righteous living rather than creeds and correct beliefs.

As you read, consider the following questions:
1. What are the Vedas and of what importance are they in the Hindu belief system, according to Radhakrishnan?
2. According to the author, why do Hindus "vary continually" their notions of God?
3. What are the attributes of the "truly religious," in Radhakrishnan's opinion?

Sarvepalli Radhakrishnan, *The Hindu View of Life*. Basingstoke, England: Macmillan, Inc., 1926.

The Hindu attitude to religion is interesting. While fixed intellectual beliefs mark off one religion from another, Hinduism sets itself no such limits. Intellect is subordinated to intuition, dogma to experience, outer expression to inward realization. Religion is not the acceptance of academic abstractions or the celebration of ceremonies, but a kind of life or experience. It is insight into the nature of reality (*darsana*), or experience of reality (*anubhava*). This experience is not an emotional thrill, or a subjective fancy, but is the response of the whole personality, the integrated self to the central reality. Religion is a specific attitude of the self, itself and no other, though it is mixed up generally with intellectual views, aesthetic forms, and moral valuations. . . .

The Vedas

The chief sacred scriptures of the Hindus, the Vedas, register the intuitions of the perfected souls. They are not so much dogmatic dicta as transcripts from life. They record the spiritual experiences of souls strongly endowed with the sense for reality. They are held to be authoritative on the ground that they express the experiences of the experts in the field of religion. If the utterances of the Vedas were uninformed by spiritual insight, they would have no claim to our belief. The truths revealed in the Vedas are capable of being re-experienced on compliance with ascertained conditions. . . .

The Hindu philosophy of religion starts from and returns to an experimental basis. Only this basis is as wide as human nature itself. Other religious systems start with this or that particular experimental datum. Christian theology, for example, takes its stand on the immediate certitude of Jesus as one whose absolute authority over conscience is self-certifying and whose ability and willingness to save the soul it is impossible not to trust. Christian theology becomes relevant only for those who share or accept a particular kind of spiritual experience, and these are tempted to dismiss other experiences as illusory and other scriptures as imperfect. Hinduism was not betrayed into this situation on account of its adherence to fact. The Hindu thinker readily admits other points of view than his own and considers them to be just as worthy of attention. If the whole race of man, in ev-

111

ery land, of every colour, and every stage of culture is the offspring of God, then we must admit that, in the vast compass of his providence, all are being trained by his wisdom and supported by his love to reach within the limits of their powers a knowledge of the Supreme. When the Hindu found that different people aimed at and achieved God-realization in different ways, he generously recognized them all and justified their place in the course of history. He used the distinctive scriptures of the different groups for their uplift since they remain the source, almost the only source, for the development of their tastes and talents for the enrichment of their thought and life, for the appeal to their emotions and the inspiration of their efforts. . . .

The Nature of God

It is sometimes urged that the descriptions of God conflict with one another. It only shows that our notions are not true. To say that our ideas of God are not true is not to deny the reality of God to which our ideas refer. Refined definitions of God as moral personality, and holy love may contradict cruder ones which look upon Him as a primitive despot, a sort of sultan in the sky, but they all intend the same reality. . . .

When asked to define the nature of God, the seer of the Upanisad sat silent, and when pressed to answer exclaimed that the Absolute is silence, *santa 'yam atma*. The mystery of the divine reality eludes the machinery of speech and symbol. The "Divine Darkness," "That of which nothing can be said," and such other expressions are used by the devout when they attempt to describe their consciousness of direct communion with God.

The Hindu thinkers bring out the sense of the otherness of the divine by the use of negatives, "There the eye goes not, speech goes not, nor mind, we know not, we understand not how one would teach it.". . .

Hindu thought believes in the evolution of our knowledge of God. We have to vary continually our notions of God until we pass beyond all notions into the heart of the reality itself, which our ideas endeavour to report. Hinduism does not distinguish ideas of God as true and false, adopting one

The Divine Reality

Brahman, the nonpersonal Supreme One, pervades all things and transcends all things. Of this great Principle, the Rig Veda states, "Though men call it by many names, it is really One." An essential part of the teaching regarding Brahman is the belief that a man can, by personal effort, and use of inner knowledge, attain union with this Divine One while still on earth. Such blissful union is made possible because the Ultimate Reality and the individual soul (*atman*), though seemingly apart, are, in actuality, one and the same substance. This identity of soul and God in Hinduism is given terse expression in an often-quoted Sanskrit formula: *Tat tvam asi*, or "That art Thou.". . .

The attainment of individual mystic union with the Divine Reality which exists eternally behind the world's ever-changing maya [the world our senses experience] is Hinduism's highest aim, and it cannot be too often repeated that this belief in one supreme Divinity serves to place Hinduism among monotheistic world faiths, in spite of its bewildering acceptance, on certain levels, of devotional practices polytheistic or animistic in nature.

Nancy Wilson Ross, *Three Ways of Asian Wisdom*, 1966.

---

particular idea as the standard for the whole human race. It accepts the obvious fact that mankind seeks its goal of God at various levels and in various directions, and feels sympathy with every stage of the search. The same God expresses itself at one stage as power, at another as personality, at a third as all-comprehensive spirit, just as the same forces which put forth the green leaves also cause the crimson flower to grow. We do not say that the crimson flowers are all the truth and the green leaves are all false. Hinduism accepts all religious notions as facts and arranges them in the order of their more or less intrinsic significance. The bewildering polytheism of the masses and the uncompromising monotheism of the classes are for the Hindu the expressions of one and the same force at different levels. Hinduism insists on our working steadily upwards and improving our knowledge of God.

"The worshippers of the Absolute are the highest in rank; second to them are the worshippers of the personal God; then come the worshippers of the incarnations like Rama, Krsna,

Buddha; below them are those who worship ancestors, deities and sages, and lowest of all are the worshippers of the petty forces and spirits." Again, "The deities of some men are in water (i.e., bathing places), those of the child (in religion) are in images of wood and stone, but the sage finds his God in his deeper self." "The man of action finds his God in fire, the man of feeling in the heart, and the feeble-minded in the idol, but the strong in spirit find God everywhere." The seers see the Supreme in the self, and not in images. . . .

Hinduism developed an attitude of comprehensive charity instead of a fanatic faith in an inflexible creed. It accepted the multiplicity of aboriginal gods and others which originated, most of them outside the Aryan tradition, and justified them all. It brought together into one whole all believers in God. Many sects professing many different beliefs live within the Hindu fold. Heresy-hunting, the favourite game of many religions, is singularly absent from Hinduism.

Acceptance of Other Faiths

Hinduism is wholly free from the strange obsession of the Semitic faiths that the acceptance of a particular religious metaphysic is necessary for salvation, and nonacceptance thereof is a heinous sin meriting eternal punishment in hell. . . .

After all, what counts is not creed but conduct. By their fruits ye shall know them and not by their beliefs. Religion is not correct belief but righteous living. The truly religious never worry about other people's beliefs. Look at the great saying of Jesus: Other sheep I have which are not of this fold." Jesus was born a Jew and died a Jew. He did not tell the Jewish people among whom he found himself, "It is wicked to be Jews. Become Christians." He did his best to rid the Jewish religion of its impurities. He would have done the same with Hinduism were he born a Hindu. The true reformer purifies and enlarges the heritage of mankind and does not belittle, still less deny it.

Those who love their sects more than truth end by loving themselves more than their sects. We start by claiming that Christianity is the only true religion and then affirm that Protestantism is the only true sect of Christianity, Episcopalianism the only true Protestantism, the High Church the only true Episcopal Protestant Christian religion, and our particular standpoint the only true representation of the High Church View.

The Hindu theory that every human being, every group and every nation has an individuality worthy of reverence is slowly gaining ground. Such a view requires that we should allow absolute freedom to every group to cultivate what is most distinctive and characteristic of it. All peculiarity is unique and incommunicable, and it will be to disregard the nature of reality to assume that what is useful to one will be useful to everyone else to the same extent. The world is wide enough to hold men whose natures are different.

"By following the Buddhist path we aim to awaken to our true nature, the enlightened qualities of a Buddha."

Buddhism Seeks Enlightenment and Ultimate Reality

Gill Farrer-Halls

Rather than being a religion in which a creator god is worshipped, Buddhism is a way of life that emphasizes meditation, renunciation of possessions and pleasures, and the cultivation of compassion and wisdom, Gill Farrer-Halls explains in the following viewpoint. By following the teachings of the Buddha, developing inner strength, and facing difficulties with like-minded spiritual friends and teachers, we can ultimately reach a state of enlightenment known as nirvana, the author writes. At rest in nirvana, one is free from suffering and illusion and can choose to abandon the cycle of birth and rebirth or to enter the world to benefit others. Farrer-Halls is the author of *The Illustrated Encyclopedia of Buddhist Wisdom*, from which this viewpoint is excerpted.

As you read, consider the following questions:
1. In the author's opinion, what is the purpose of renunciation?
2. What are the Three Jewels of Buddhism, according to Farrer-Halls?
3. According to the author, what are the five mental states that hinder spiritual progress?

Gill Farrer-Halls, *The Illustrated Encyclopedia of Buddhist Wisdom*. Wheaton, IL: Quest Books, 2000. Copyright © 2000 by Quest Books. Reproduced by permission.

Buddhism is not a belief system or an abstract philosophy. It is a way of life, with teachings on how to behave and qualities to cultivate. Its methodology is meditation, something we practice rather than study. By following the Buddhist path we aim to awaken to our true nature, the enlightened qualities of a Buddha.

Prince Siddhartha [the founder of Buddhism] renounced all his possessions and pleasures, and we too need to develop a sense of renunciation. Luckily, this does not necessarily mean abandoning everything and living in a cave for years! Though, if this is what we choose, we are following a pure and authentic Buddhist path.

Renunciation means lessening both our attachment to those things we like and our aversion to unpleasant situations and feelings, by realizing that none of these things have an inherent ability to make us happy or unhappy.

Dealing with Desire and Aversion

As Buddhists we can still have nice things and enjoy them, but when they are taken away, we accept it and do not get upset. We try not to be greedy or to seek too hard to satisfy our desires. We can learn to live with and accept our desires without the obsession to satisfy them immediately. At the same time, we can learn to accept disagreeable things without fighting against them. We can rest in the knowledge that whatever bothers us is impermanent and will pass.

A tightly closed fist tries to grasp hold of things, but they slip away because of this grasping. If we open our hands, things pour over and move on unimpeded. In this way, by not trying to control the natural flow of life, we can enjoy it. When we loosen our grasping we become open, which makes us receptive to our environment. We can appreciate other people and our surroundings beyond our tightly held perceptions.

Everyone seeks happiness but as Shakyamuni Buddha said, "There is no way to happiness—happiness is the way." Living a life guided by compassion and wisdom will help us to find happiness in the here and now.

When we first encounter Buddha's teachings the ideas can seem so wonderful that we think being a Buddhist will make us special or different in some way. But, we should not lose sight of the ordinary; we are normal and share the same nature as all other beings. The only difference is that we have the opportunity to awaken to our buddhanature through listening to the teachings and applying them in our lives. Therefore we do not have to dress differently, or shave our heads, or appear different from others—unless we choose to become a nun or a monk.

Being vegetarian is an appropriate expression of the Buddha's teaching on not harming others, but it is not essential. Diet is culturally conditioned. Tibetans eat meat because it is difficult to grow vegetables in their climate. Theravada Buddhists depend on alms and therefore eat whatever they are given. Chinese Buddhists, and Buddhists in the traditions that developed from Ch'an, such as Korean, are usually strictly vegetarian.

We must each choose for ourselves whether to be vegetarian or not. Food in the West is plentiful. This has caused obsession over food, reflected in diseases like bulimia and anorexia. Buddhism emphasises a middle way approach, eating moderately, and this is perhaps most important.

Death, Enlightenment, and Nirvana

Buddhism is sometimes thought to be gloomy and pessimistic because it teaches us to look at the inevitability of death. However, realizing we will die encourages us to make the most of our lives. Then we investigate what Buddha said would make us happy and try to live according to his teachings.

Buddhism is not a theistic religion, and Buddha was not a creator God, as in Christianity. Nirvana is not heaven; it is a state of enlightenment that can be experienced here and now. An enlightened being—a Buddha, or Bodhisattva—can rest in Nirvana or purposefully enter the world to benefit all other beings. Thus Nirvana is not a place, it is the extinguishing of suffering, delusion, and craving.

The Three Jewels

When we commit ourselves to the Buddhist path, we first take refuge in the Three Jewels. This means relying upon them for guidance. Normally we take refuge in external objects—for example, when we are hungry we take refuge in food—but these bring only temporary satisfaction. The Buddha, Dharma, and Sangha are inner resources, and are reliable objects of refuge.

Mindful Meditation

In Buddhism, our effort is to practice mindfulness in each moment—to know what is going on within and all around us. When the Buddha was asked, "Sir, what do you and your monks practice?" he replied, "we sit, we walk, and we eat." The questioner continued, "But sir, everyone sits, walks, and eats," and the Buddha told him, "When we sit, we *know* we are sitting. When we walk, we *know* we are walking. When we eat, we *know* we are eating." Most of the time, we are lost in the past or carried away by future projects and concerns. When we are mindful, touching deeply the present moment, we can see and listen deeply, and the fruits are always understanding, acceptance, love, and the desire to relieve suffering and bring joy. . . .

There are many conflicting feelings and ideas within us, and it is important for us to look deeply and know what is going on. When there are wars within us, it will not be long before we are at war with others, even those we love. . . . If we go back to ourselves and touch our feelings, we will see the ways that we furnish the fuel for the wars going on inside. Meditation is, first of all, a tool for surveying our own territory so we can know what is going on. With the energy of mindfulness, we can calm things down, understand them, and bring harmony back to the conflicting elements inside us. If we can learn ways to touch the peace, joy, and happiness that are already there, we will become healthy and strong, and a resource for others.

Thich Nhat Hanh, *Living Buddha, Living Christ*, 1995.

We take refuge in the Buddha because he has gone beyond suffering and developed great wisdom and compassion. Buddha has no partiality and wishes to help everyone, no matter who they are or what they have done. There are as many ways to teach people as there are human dispositions, so the Buddha can guide each individual according to need. Refuge in the Buddha alludes to being open to and relying upon the limitless love, compassion, and wisdom of those who have attained enlightenment. It also means cultivating our own potential buddhanature, seeds of enlightenment within us.

In order to be free of suffering, we must first know what it is and understand what the causes are. This means training our minds by following the teachings. We take refuge in the Dharma,[1] the true protection from suffering, by developing wisdom from our study and practice of the Buddha's teachings.

Refuge in the Dharma is trusting that the teachings of the Buddha will ultimately lead us to enlightenment, by following the methods he taught. It also means developing our own inner wisdom that tells us what is right and wrong.

Without inspiration from our more advanced spiritual friends and teachers, we are likely to experience many disheartening problems that make it difficult to maintain our Dharma practice and meditation. So we take refuge in the Sangha and follow their example when we have problems.

Refuge in the Sangha refers to our spiritual friends. By talking together we can share experiences, find answers to questions, and resolve problems. Meditating together is inspiring and develops faith. Refuge in the Sangha is also recognizing that we too can help our friends.

To take refuge fully in the Three Jewels we need to cultivate two qualities of mind. We must first really wish to be free from suffering. We can think of this in terms of our current life or of not being reborn in the lower realms in future lives. We must also sincerely believe that the Three Jewels can help us. Then we have really taken refuge.

The Wheel of Life

The Wheel of Life depicts how we are trapped in samsara.[2] At the center of the Wheel are three animals, symbolic of the three poisons. They are shown head to tail eating each other, which symbolizes endless cycles of suffering, with one poison causing the next.

The pig represents ignorance, blindness, and delusion. This refers to our erroneous perception of how the world exists; we believe things exist independently and provide

1. the Way of Truth   2. the cycle of birth and rebirth

lasting satisfaction. We also believe that we exist concretely, rather than in dependence on our different components and external conditions.

This ignorance of how things exist leads to desire, represented by the cock. We mistakenly believe a desired object will bring us enduring happiness. So desire, craving, and lust arise, which cause us suffering, because no sooner do we get what we want than we want something else.

Unsatisfied desire leads to hatred and anger, symbolized by the snake. Because we believe ourselves to exist independently, we place fulfilling our own desires above the well-being of others. So when we don't get what we want, we feel hatred or anger toward someone who has the object we crave.

Anger and hatred prevent us from thinking clearly. So when we suffer these feelings we are unable to change our erroneous perception of how things exist, which keeps us in ignorance. . . .

Is there an end to this self-perpetuating suffering? If we look . . . we see Buddha at the top left, standing outside the Wheel of Life pointing to the moon. He symbolizes liberation from ignorance, desire, and hatred—the causes of suffering. Taking refuge in the Three Jewels helps free us from the three poisons and the five hindrances.

The Five Hindrances

Buddha described five mental states which hinder our spiritual progress and perpetuate suffering. They are: (1) sensual desire, (2) ill will, (3) sloth and torpor, (4) worry and restlessness, and (5) confused doubt.

As well as following the Buddha's path generally, we can also apply specific remedies. For instance, if we feel overwhelming desire for another person, we can lessen our suffering by meditating on the repulsive nature of his or her body. We can visualize what the body is composed of and that it will decompose at death. We can consciously direct goodwill at someone toward whom we feel ill will. We can meditate that this person also wishes to be happy and avoid suffering, just as we do.

Sloth and torpor are best overcome by eating less and taking more exercise. Worry and restlessness often arise from an

uneasy conscience, so repenting any negative actions and re-
solving to not do them again lessens worry. This is the purpose of Catholic confession and psychotherapy, both summed
up with the saying "a problem shared is a problem halved."

Confused doubt, as opposed to skeptical questioning,
which is useful, is best cured by further practice and study of
Buddha's teachings. As we saw with worry, talking things
over with like-minded spiritual friends can help clarify particular issues and help you make positive decisions.

| *"Let us reaffirm our ancient covenant, our sacred bond with our Mother, the Goddess of nature and spirituality."*

Ecofeminism Reclaims the Great Mother Goddess

Riane Eisler

Riane Eisler is the author of the international bestseller *The Chalice and the Blade* and the cofounder of the Center for Partnership Studies, a research and educational center in Pacific Grove, California. In her works Eisler reinterprets ancient history and modern archaeological findings to support ecofeminism, a philosophy that advocates living in sexual and social equality and in harmony with nature. According to Eisler, humans should reject current male-dominated, warlike cultures and return to the egalitarian societal model of the past, which she feels is the true path of human cultural evolution. To do so, she argues, we must rediscover and reaffirm the ancient Mother Goddess, who represents the feminine aspect of the divine and the union of nature and spirituality.

As you read, consider the following questions:

1. What is the Gaia hypothesis, according to Eisler?
2. In the author's opinion, why is matriarchy not a suitable alternative to patriarchy?
3. Which ancient goddesses express the "spirituality, mercy, wisdom, and justice" of the Mother Goddess, according to Eisler?

Riane Eisler, "The Gaia Tradition and the Partnership Future—an Ecofeminist Manifesto," *Reweaving the World*, edited by Irene Diamond and Gloria F. Orenstein. San Francisco: Sierra Club Books, 1990. Copyright © 1990 by Sierra Club Books. Reproduced by permission of the editors.

The leading-edge social movements of our time—the peace, feminist, and ecology movements, and ecofeminism, which integrates all three—are in some respects very new. But they also draw from very ancient traditions only now being reclaimed due to what British archaeologist James Mellaart calls a veritable revolution in archaeology.

These traditions go back thousands of years. Scientific archaeological methods are now making it possible to document the way people lived and thought in prehistoric times. One fascinating discovery about our past is that for millennia—a span of time many times longer than the 5,000 years conventionally counted as history—prehistoric societies worshipped the Goddess of nature and spirituality, our great Mother, the giver of life and creator of all. But even more fascinating is that these ancient societies were structured very much like the more peaceful and just society we are now trying to construct.

A Reverence for the Earth

This is not to say that these were ideal societies or utopias. But, unlike our societies, they were *not* warlike. They were *not* societies where women were subordinate to men. And they did *not* see our Earth as an object for exploitation and domination.

In short, they were societies that had what we today call an ecological consciousness: the awareness that the Earth must be treated with reverence and respect. And this reverence for the life-giving and life-sustained powers of the Earth was rooted in a social structure where women and "feminine" values such as caring, compassion, and non-violence were not subordinate to men and the so-called masculine values of conquest and domination. Rather, the life-giving powers incarnated in women's bodies were given the highest social value. . . .

The Gaia Tradition

We now know that there was not one cradle of civilization in Sumer about 3,500 years ago. Rather, there were many cradles of civilization, all of them thousands of years older. And thanks to far more scientific and extensive archaeological excavations, we also know that in these highly creative societies women held important social positions as priestesses, craftspeople, and elders of matrilineal clans. Contrary to what we have been taught of the Neolithic or first agrarian civilizations as male dominated and highly violent, these were generally peaceful societies in which both women and men lived in harmony with one another and nature. Moreover, in all these peaceful cradles of civilization, to borrow Merlin Stone's arresting phrase from the book of the same title, "God was a woman" (New York: Dial Press, 1976).

The Goddess Rather than God

I used to think of the divine as "God." Now, if I think in terms of a personalized deity at all, I think more of the Goddess than of the God. I feel very strongly that our society's denial of the feminine aspect of the deity, the Mother aspect, is one of the great obstacles to having that personal relationship, that direct connection with the divine.

Riane Eisler, *For the Love of God,* 1990.

There is today much talk about the Gaia hypothesis (so called because Gaia is the Greek name for the Earth). This is a new scientific theory proposed by biologists Lynn Margulis and James Lovelock that our planet is a living system designed to maintain and to nurture life. But what is most striking about the Gaia hypothesis is that in essence it is a scientific update of the belief system of Goddess-worshipping prehistoric societies. In these societies the world was viewed as the great Mother, a living entity who in both her temporal and spiritual manifestations creates and nurtures all forms of life. . . .

Dominator and Partnership Societies

Even in the nineteenth century, when archaeology was still in its infancy, scholars found evidence of societies where women were not subordinate to men. But their interpretation of this evidence was that if these societies were not patriarchies, they must have been matriarchies. In other words, if men did not dominate women, then women must have dominated men. However, this conclusion is not borne out by the evidence. Rather, it is a function of what I have called a *dominator* society worldview. The real alternative to patriarchy is not matriarchy, which is only the other side of the dominator coin. The alternative, now revealed to be the original direction of our cultural evolution, is what I call a *partnership* society: a way of organizing human relations in which beginning with the most fundamental difference in our species—the difference between female and male—diversity is *not* equated with inferiority or superiority.

What we have until now been taught as history is only the history of dominator species—the record of the male dominant, authoritarian, and highly violent civilizations that began about 5,000 years ago. For example, the conventional view is that the beginning of European civilization is marked by the emergence in ancient Greece of the Indo-Europeans. But the new archaeological evidence demonstrates that the arrival of the Indo-Europeans actually marks the truncation of European civilization. That is, as Marija Gimbutas extensively documents, there was in Greece and the Balkans an earlier civilization, which she calls the civilization of Old Europe (*The Goddesses and Gods of Old Europe*, 1982). The first Indo-European invasions (by pastoralists from the arid steppes of the northeast) foreshadow the end of a matrifocal, matrilineal, peaceful agrarian era. Like fingerprints in the archaeological record, we see evidence of how wave after wave of barbarian invaders from the barren fringes of the globe leave in their wake destruction and what archaeologists call cultural impoverishment. And what characterizes these invaders is that they bring with them male dominance along with their angry gods of thunder and war. . . .

The Goddess Was the Source of All Life

We have been taught that in "Western tradition," religion is the spiritual realm and that spirituality is separate from, and superior to, nature. But for our Goddess-worshipping ancestors, spirituality and nature were one. In the religion of Western partnership societies, there was no need for the artificial distinction between spirituality and nature or for the exclusion of half of humanity from spiritual power.

In sharp contrast to "traditional" patriarchal religions (where only men can be priests, rabbis, bishops, lamas, Zen masters, and popes), we know from Minoan, Egyptian, Sumerian, and other ancient records that women were once priest-esses. Indeed, the highest religious office appears to have been that of high priestess in service of the Goddess. And the Goddess herself was not only the source of all life and nature; she was also the font of spirituality, mercy, wisdom, and justice. For example, as the Sumerian Goddess Nanshe, she sought justice for the poor and shelter for the weak. The Egyptian Goddess Maat was also the goddess of justice. The Greek Goddess Demeter was known as the lawgiver, the bringer of civilization, dispensing mercy and justice. As the Celtic Goddess Cerridwen, she was the goddess of intelligence and knowledge. And it is Gaia, the primeval prophetess of the shrine of Delphi, who in Greek mythology is said to have given the golden apple tree (the tree of knowledge) to her daughter, the Goddess Hera. Moreover, the Greek Fates, the enforcers of laws, are female. And so also are the Greek Muses, who inspire all creative endeavor. . . .

The Feminine Aspect of the Deity

I believe that the denial of our connection with the Mother aspect, the feminine aspect of the deity, is one of the major obstacles to achieving that meaningful and fulfilling personal relationship not only with the deity but with one another. We all can observe the element of the feminine, of the Mother, of the nurturer, from our experiences of a mother. The Great Mother also has a dark aspect, however: the transformative aspect of reclaiming life at death. But to have been deprived of that motherly dimension in the deity reflects something in our dominator society: a deadening of empathy, a deadening of caring, a denial of the feminine in men, and a contempt for women and the feminine.

Riane Eisler, *For the Love of God*, 1990.

We also know from a number of contemporary tribal societies that the separation between nature and spirituality is not universal. Tribal peoples generally think of nature in spiritual terms. Nature spirits must be respected, indeed, revered. And we also know that in many of these tribal societies women as well as men can be shamans or spiritual healers and that descent in these tribes is frequently traced through the mother.

In sum, *both* nature and woman can partake of spirituality in societies oriented to a partnership model. In such societies there is no need for a false dichotomy between a "masculine" spirituality and "feminine" nature. Moreover, since in ancient partnership societies woman and the Goddess were identified with *both* nature and spirituality, neither woman nor nature were devalued and exploited. . . .

We Must Rediscover the Goddess of Spirituality

For many thousands of years, millennia longer than the 5,000 years we count as recorded history, everything was done in a sacred manner. Planting and harvesting fields were rites of spring and autumn celebrated in a ritual way. Baking bread from grains, molding pots out of clay, weaving cloth out of fibers, carving tools out of metals—all these ways of technologically melding culture and nature were sacred ceremonies. There was then no splintering of culture and nature, spirituality, science, and technology. Both our intuition and our reason were applied to the building of civilization, to devising better ways for us to live and work cooperatively.

The rediscovery of these traditions signals a way out of our alienation from one another and from nature. In our time, when the nuclear bomb and advanced technology threaten all life on this planet, the reclamation of these traditions can be the basis for the restructuring of society: the completion of the modern transformation from a dominator to a partnership world.

Poised on the brink of ecocatastrophe, let us gain the courage to look at the world anew, to reverse custom, to transcend our limitations, to break free from the conventional constraints, the conventional views of what are knowledge and truth. Let us understand that we cannot graft peace and ecological balance on a dominator system; that a just and egalitarian society is impossible without the full and equal partnership of women and men.

Let us reaffirm our ancient covenant, our sacred bond with our Mother, the Goddess of nature and spirituality. Let us renounce the worship of angry gods wielding thunderbolts or swords. Let us once again honor the chalice, the ancient symbol of the power to create and enhance life—and let us understand that this power is not woman's alone but also man's.

A Renewed Understanding

For ourselves, and for the sake of our children and their children, let us use our human thrust for creation rather than destruction. Let us teach our sons and daughters that men's conquest of nature, of women, and of other men is not a heroic virtue; that we have the knowledge and the capacity to survive; that we need not blindly follow our bloodstained path to planetary death; that we can reawaken from our 5,000-year dominator nightmare and allow our evolution to resume its interrupted course.

While there is still time, let us fulfill our promise. Let us reclaim the trees of knowledge and of life. Let us regain our lost sense of wonder and reverence for the miracles of life and love, let us learn again to live in partnership so we may fulfill our responsibility to ourselves and to our Great Mother, this wondrous planet Earth.

"There is a desperate need for spirituality in our time, yet this spirituality must be in dialogue and communion with everything of value in our mystical and religious traditions."

Interspirituality Embraces the Heart of All Religions

Wayne Teasdale

Wayne Teasdale was an interreligious monk who combined the traditions of Catholicism and Hinduism. An activist and teacher involved in building common ground between religions, Teasdale served on the board of the Parliament of the World's Religions and was a member of the Monastic Interreligious Dialogue before his death in 2004. In the following viewpoint, excerpted from his book *The Mystic Heart*, Teasdale defines interspirituality, a comprehensive approach to faith that draws on the inner truths of the world's religious traditions. When we openly and respectfully share the spiritual treasures of our diverse traditions, Teasdale writes, a greater truth can be realized. He believes that interfaith dialogue can transform the heart of humanity, enabling us to transcend the violence and division of our history and build a just and peaceful civilization.

As you read, consider the following questions:
1. What shifts in human understanding reveal the birth of a new awareness, in Teasdale's opinion?
2. Why does Teasdale use the word *Pentecost* to describe the August 1993 Parliament of the World's Religions?
3. What is "the definitive revolution," in the author's opinion?

We are at the dawn of a new consciousness, a radically fresh approach to our life as the human family in a fragile world. This birth into a new awareness, into a new set of historical circumstances, appears in a number of shifts in our understanding:

The emergence of ecological awareness and sensitivity to the natural, organic world, with an acknowledgment of the basic fragility of the earth.

A growing sense of the rights of other species.

A recognition of the interdependence of all domains of life and reality.

The ideal of abandoning a militant nationalism as a result of this tangible sense of our essential interdependence.

A deep, evolving experience of community between and among the religions through their individual members.

The growing receptivity to the inner treasures of the world's religions.

An openness to the cosmos, with the realization that the relationship between humans and the earth is part of the larger community of the universe.

Each of these shifts represents dramatic change; taken together, they will define the thought and culture of the third millennium. Fewer and fewer people are questioning the vital importance of the environmental issue. Its significance is so great that Thomas Berry—who refers to himself as a *geologian*, or a theologian for the earth—believes in naming this new period in history the *Ecological* or *Ecozoic Age*. We could really name the age after any of these shifts in understanding. To encompass them all, however, perhaps the best name for this new segment of historical experience is the *Interspiritual Age*.

Preparing for a Universal Civilization

All of these awarenesses are interrelated, and each is indispensable to clearly grasping the greater shift taking place, a shift that will sink roots deep into our lives and culture. Taken together, they are preparing the way for a universal civilization: a civilization with a *heart*. Such a universal society will draw its inspiration from perennial spiritual and moral insights, intuitions, and experiences. These aspects of spirituality will shape how we conduct politics and education; how we envision our economies, media, and entertainment; and how we develop our relationship with the natural world, while pursuing our quality of life.

The awakening to our ecological interconnectedness, with its concomitant sense of the preciousness of all other species, raises the earth to where it becomes the center of our moral, aesthetic, economic, political, social, cultural, and spiritual activities. We have to learn to negotiate the balance between the individual and the totality, rather than erring too far to one side, as in the past. Negative forms of nationalism and tribalism are beyond redemption. They need to be firmly set aside. In their extreme expressions, they poison the earth's common good, as we have seen in Iraq, Iran, Yugoslavia, Rwanda, and elsewhere. As we become more aware of our intrinsic interdependence, destructive nationalism will pass away, and a more positive approach to nationhood as a cohesive force within a democratic system will take hold.

Interdependence

Interdependence is an inescapable fact of our contemporary world. Not only is it a prevailing condition that dominates international commerce, cultural exchange, and scientific collaboration, it is a value that promotes stable global peace. The more the bonds of interconnectedness define the shape and scope of the future, the less likely they will be ruptured. The more interdependent we are, the more we will safeguard the system of the universal society.

A *spiritual* interdependence also exists between and among the world's religions. This interdependence is more subtle, though the actual impact of traditions on each other is clearly discernible in history, particularly where cultural contiguity exists. Hinduism has directly influenced the rise of Buddhism, for example. Jainism, in its teaching of *ahimsa*, or nonharming, has influenced both Buddhism and Hinduism. Christianity would hardly be possible without Judaism, and Islam is inconceivable without these predecessors. Sikhism developed in North India in the sixteenth century as a reaction to Islamic persecution, but its religious life, beliefs, rituals, and spirituality were shaped by both

Hindu and Muslim forms. Similarly, Confucianism and Taoism in China mutually influenced each other, and Taoism had a deep impact on Ch'an Buddhism, which became Zen in Japan. These are just a few examples. Endless studies demonstrate the impact of earlier, lesser-known traditions and myths on the development and doctrines of the historical faiths. The impact of myths and these other traditions on the biblical tradition alone is staggering. . . .

When we examine relations among the religions today, we find traditions increasingly discovering and pursuing a real experience of community, especially among individuals. This existential realization arises from actual encounters between people of differing traditions. Throughout history, members of different traditions have entered deep, meaningful dialogues, which arose out of amicable relations between communities. The third-century reign of the Buddhist Emperor Asoka of the Mauran Dynasty in India, for example, was enormously welcoming of other traditions. Asoka practiced tolerance and respect, stimulating interfaith encounters. India, alone, has many examples of interfaith encounter.

The Parliament of the World's Religions

Most of recorded history, however, chronicles thousands of years of isolation. Cultures of separation have clung to an exclusivist perspective that has left no room for other traditions. The attitude of exclusivity is both distrustful of other faiths and disrespectful of their insights and experiences. There is no basis for dialogue, let alone a bond of community.

One of the special historical moments of breakthrough, however, occurred in 1893 when the World's Parliament of Religions was convoked in Chicago. The Parliament met for seventeen days in September as one of twenty-four congresses of the World Columbian Exposition, or world's fair. It brought the planet's religions together for the first time in the modern age. It wasn't completely inclusive: Native Americans, other indigenous peoples, and African Americans were excluded, and only one Muslim, an American convert, was present as a delegate. But it had a profound impact, capturing the imagination of the American people and the world press. It reinforced the study of comparative religion and helped make Catholicism and Judaism mainstream in America, while introducing the Asian religions to the West, especially Hinduism, Jainism, Buddhism, and Zen.

Many early attempts to solidify the spirit of the Parliament in a permanent organization failed. But a number of organizations carried on the work, including the Fellowship of Reconciliation, the World Conference on Religion and Peace, the World Congress of Faiths, the Temple of Understanding, the Council for a Parliament of the World's Religions, and the United Religions Organization. Today, these groups collaborate on dialogue programs, and other projects of mutual concern. All the major cities of the world also have interfaith organizations: New York, Chicago, Los Angeles, San Francisco, Washington, Seattle, Denver, Austin, Toronto, Victoria, London, Paris, Madrid, Berlin, Tokyo, New Delhi, Madras, Bombay, Jerusalem, Ankara, and Moscow are all centers of interreligious encounter.

In August 1993, the Council for a Parliament of the World's Religions, founded in 1988, convened the Parliament of the World's Religions in Chicago. Initially designed to commemorate the centennial of the first great Parliament, the founders quickly realized that they had an opportunity to contribute something more substantial—to address the critical issues plaguing the planet: the environmental crisis, social injustice, poverty, malnutrition, disease, the plight of refugees—80 percent of whom are women and children—the need for better education in developing nations, and numerous other threats to peace. . . .

A Second Pentecost

Sessions ranged from the colorful opening to explorations of the inner life, interreligious dialogue, memories of paradise, the next generation, the dispossessed, contributions of the imagination, seminars on all the religions, spiritual teachings by great masters, academic symposia, dance workshops, twice daily meditation sessions, lectures on virtually every aspect of religious knowledge, forums dedicated to ecology, and more than a thousand other programs involving spiritual practice. In a bow to tradition, the 250-member Assembly of Religious and Spiritual Leaders gathered for a three-day meeting at the Art Institute. These stormy sessions ended well when two hundred members signed the Parliament's document *Towards a Global Ethic (An Initial Declaration)*, the first consensus by the world's religions on basic standards of ethical behavior.

A Special Message to the Young

You must stand up on your own two feet in the spiritual life. You are responsible for this process; it cannot be shifted to your parents, your friends, or your teachers. You have to embrace the spiritual journey, and you are the one who has to be transformed. . . . You must find your own way, and you must be faithful to the truth you know or discover.

As you look to your parents or friends for guidance, ask yourself: "Are they good examples of the spiritual life? Are they serious about their own development or transformation, or are they wasting time on activities that distract them from the work of life?" If they are serious about the spiritual dimension of existence, learn what you can from them. If their commitment is to a religious tradition, then respect it; try to integrate it. But if it doesn't include authentic spirituality, and it isn't open to other traditions, then discover your own path and find your own spirituality.

Look to all traditions of the spiritual life and adopt an attitude of interspirituality. Claim the wisdom dimension of all the traditions for yourself, and let wisdom guide you. If you find your parents' approach lacking, don't reject it; rather, build on it. If their position is wanting, approach them with compassion. Perhaps you can teach them something!

Wayne Teasdale, *The Mystic Heart*, 1999.

The Parliament represented the most diverse group of people ever to meet in one place in the history of humankind. Before the event's eight days, I assisted in the planning and served on four committees. During the Parliament itself, I participated in a number of forums, including the Buddhist-Christian Monastic Dialogue with the Dalai Lama and in the Assembly. I hoped, prayed, and even knew intuitively that it would represent a turning point. But it greatly exceeded everyone's expectations. . . .

Something extraordinary happened during the Parliament's days. The divine showed up and opened everyone, inspiring enthusiasm, mutual trust, receptivity, and a wonderful sense of joy, spontaneity, community, and urgency. We were not of one mind but of one heart. For me as a Christian, the word that best describes this historic moment is *Pentecost:* the birth of the Christian church, when the Holy Spirit opened the minds and hearts of Jesus' disciples, uniting them in a corporate mystical knowing that illumined their path during the fledgling years of the apostolic age. The Parliament represented a second Pentecost because the spirit was tangibly present, prying hearts and minds open to receive the impulse of new vision. Community was born among the religions. The spirit gave us a whole new paradigm of relationship in the existential experience of community, replacing the old model of separation, mistrust, competition, hostility, and conflict. By supplanting the approach responsible for thousands of wars throughout human history, this new paradigm has enormous meaning. The advent of community between and among members of differing faiths is without parallel; its opportunity is extremely precious, not to be squandered but carefully cultivated and applied to the task of building a universal civilization.

Cross-Religious Sharing

Interspirituality and intermysticism are the terms I have coined to designate the increasingly familiar phenomenon of cross-religious sharing of interior resources, the spiritual treasures of each tradition. Of course everyone isn't participating; really it is only a minority, but its members are the more mystically developed in each tradition, and they each hold great influence. In the third millennium, interspirituality and intermysticism will become more and more the norm in humankind's inner evolution. Europeans often say a person isn't truly educated until they know more than one language. This can also be said of religions: a person is not really fully educated, or indeed "religious," unless they are intimately aware of more than their own faith and ways of prayer. . . .

Religion and spirituality are not mutually exclusive, but there is a real difference. The term spirituality refers to an individual's solitary search for and discovery of the absolute or the divine. It involves direct mystical experience of God, or realization of vast awareness, as in Buddhism. Spirituality carries with it a conviction that the transcendent is real, and it requires some sort of spiritual practice that acts as a catalyst to inner change and growth. It is primarily personal, but it also has a social dimension. Spirituality, like religion, derives from mysticism.

The Mystical Tradition

For thousands of years before the dawn of the world religions as social organisms working their way through history, the mystical life thrived. This mystical tradition, which underpins all genuine faith, is the living source of religion itself. It is the attempt to possess the inner reality of the spiritual life, with its mystical, or direct, access to the divine. Each great religion has a similar origin: the spiritual awakening of its founders to God, the divine, the absolute, the spirit, Tao, boundless awareness. We find it in the experience of the rishis in India; the Buddha in his experience of enlightenment; in Moses, the patriarchs, the prophets, and other holy souls of the biblical tradition. It is no less present in Jesus' inner realization of his relationship with his Father, who is also our Father. And it is clear in the Prophet Mohammed's revelation experience of Allah through the mediation of the Archangel Gabriel.

Everything stems from mysticism, or primary religious experience, whether it be revelation or a personal mystical state of consciousness. It is therefore quite natural and appropriate that spirituality should become more primary for people as they grow in their traditions and discover more substantial and ultimate nourishment in the living reality of the source. We need religion, yet we need direct contact with the divine, or ultimate mystery, even more. Religions are valuable carriers of the tradition within a community, but they must not be allowed to choke out the breath of the spirit, which breathes where it will.

For example, most Christian churches barely mention the mystical life, keeping the focus of prayer on the level of worship and devotion. The same is true in much of the Jewish and Islamic traditions, the Kabbalah and Sufism being exceptions. The religious life of the faithful is decidedly on the corporate, devotional level, while the contemplative and mystical are neglected.

By allowing inward change, while at the same time simplifying our external life, spirituality serves as our greatest single resource for changing our centuries-old trajectory of violence and division. Spirituality is profoundly transformative when it inspires in us the attitude of surrender to the mystery in which "we live, and move, and have our being," as the New Testament reminds us. The twentieth century has witnessed the rise and fall of so many bloody revolutions that have caused immense suffering in so many lives. The architects of these political movements defined the human in the abstract, which allowed them to destroy *living* human beings. These figures failed to see that people's hearts must change before structures can change. This change is the basis of genuine reform and renewal.

The Definitive Revolution

We need to understand, to really grasp at an elemental level, that the definitive revolution *is* the spiritual awakening of humankind. This revolution will be the task of the Interspiritual Age. The necessary shifts in consciousness require a new approach to spirituality that transcends past religious cultures of fragmentation and isolation. The direct experience of interspirituality paves the way for a universal view of mysticism—that is the common heart of the world. . . .

There is a desperate need for spirituality in our time, yet this spirituality must be in dialogue and communion with everything of value in our mystical and religious traditions. We require a spirituality that promotes the unity of the human family, not one that further divides us or maintains old antagonisms. At the same time, this interspiritual approach must not submerge our differences; it must see traditions in relationship to each other, and provide options. The truth itself is big enough to include our diversity of views. They are all based on authentic inner experience, and so are all valid.

138

CHAPTER 4

What Motivates Moral Behavior?

Chapter Preface

The news is usually brimming with stories revealing the questionable state of ethics and morals in today's world. From lying politicians and corrupt corporate practices to serial killers and genocidal wars, humankind seems to have an inexhaustible capacity for deceit and brutality. And yet even amidst such callousness, we also encounter great heroism, generosity, kindness, and honesty. Many would agree that humans have the potential to commit both good and evil. But how do we come to define what is "good" and "evil"? What enables us to choose between right and wrong?

Christian editor and author Philip Yancey, the author of the first viewpoint in this chapter, contends that humans must look beyond themselves to a higher authority for moral guidance. He believes that God—and religion, which provides a way to commune with God—constitute that moral authority. In his view, basic ethical principles are unchanging and absolute because they have been established by an absolute being, the creator of the universe. Without God, Yancey argues, we are left with the "collective sentiments of human beings" as a guide to morality, a situation which leaves us "vulnerable to dangerous swings of moral consensus." Frank R. Zindler, the editor of *American Atheist* magazine, strongly disagrees with Yancey. Zindler maintains that morality is rooted in the long-term process of human evolution and cultural development. What we now define as ethical conduct is largely learned behavior that has ensured the survival of the human species over millions of years, he writes. Zindler, then, views morality as a product of nature. In his opinion, religion is a primitive cultural adaptation that served us earlier in our evolutionary development but should now be replaced with reason.

The other authors in this chapter do not attempt to define the source of morality but rather examine worldviews and dispositions that they believe promote genuinely moral behavior. For example, humanist editor and author Paul Kurtz describes several of the principles espoused by secular humanists. Secular humanism is a philosophy that celebrates reason, freedom of thought, and individual liberty while rejecting supernaturalism and religious dogma. Kurtz maintains that rational deliberation allows us to discern what is ethical without having to rely on religious laws and authorities. Conversely, professor and author John Gray argues that secular humanism suppresses humanity's natural impulse toward religious belief. Instincts, he points out, cannot be repressed without negative consequences. Gray believes that repressed religion eventually reasserts itself in dangerous ways, resulting in tyrannies and mass atrocities.

Finally, lecturer and critic Alfie Kohn contends that altruism—an attitude of selfless concern for others—is at the root of the ability to help other people. Kohn argues that altruism stems from an inherent capacity for empathy and connectedness. However, this capacity must be developed through life experiences and encouragement from the surrounding culture. Philosopher and teacher Tibor R. Machan, on the other hand, maintains that effective moral behavior begins with self-concern. Those who have first taken care of their own needs are better able to offer assistance to others, Machan argues. He believes that the "self-sacrificing" disposition of altruism is impractical because one who does not help himself cannot successfully help others.

Philosophers, religious believers, and scientists have widely varying opinions on the origins of morality and what mental attitudes and cultural influences promote ethical behavior. The following chapter presents several of these disparate views.

"Historically, [civilization] has always relied on religion to provide a source for . . . moral authority."

Morality Requires Religious Belief

Philip Yancey

In the following viewpoint Philip Yancey contends that true morality is rooted in a belief in God. According to Yancey, contemporary secular society has reduced the notion of morality to a question of personal choice, causing a general decline in ethics. He maintains that the ability to make authentic judgments about right and wrong requires the guidance of religion; any moral system established by nonbelievers is completely arbitrary since it has no higher authority as its foundation. Yancey is the editor at large of *Christianity Today* magazine and the author of several books, including *Reaching for the Invisible God* and *What's So Amazing About Grace?*

As you read, consider the following questions:
1. How does Yancey define "unmorality"?
2. What are the symptoms of moral illness in the United States, according to Yancey?
3. According to James Davison Hunter, cited by the author, what happens to a society that loses all moral consensus?

Philip Yancey, "Nietzsche Was Right," *Books & Culture*, January/February 1998. Copyright © 1998 by Philip Yancey. Reproduced by permission.

A representative of Generation X named Sam told me he had been discovering the strategic advantages of truth. As an experiment, he decided to stop lying. "It helps people picture you and relate to you more reliably," he said. "Truth can be positively beneficial in many ways."

I asked what would happen if he found himself in a situation where it would prove *more* beneficial for him to lie. He said he would have to judge the context, but he was trying to prefer not-lying.

For Sam, the decision to lie or tell the truth involved not morality but a social construct, to be adopted or rejected as a matter of expedience. In essence, the source of moral authority for Sam is himself, and that in a nutshell is the dilemma confronting moral philosophy in the postmodern world.

The Rise of Unmorality

Something unprecedented in human history is brewing: a rejection of external moral sources altogether. Individuals and societies have always been immoral to varying degrees. Individuals (never an entire society) have sometimes declared themselves amoral, professing agnosticism about ethical matters. Only recently, however, have serious thinkers entertained the notion of unmorality: that there is no such thing as morality. A trend prefigured by [philosopher Friedrich] Nietzsche, prophesied by [writer Fyodor] Dostoyevsky, and analyzed presciently by C.S. Lewis in *The Abolition of Man* is now coming to fruition. The very concept of morality is undergoing a profound change, led in part by the advance guard of a new science called "evolutionary psychology."

So far, however, the pioneers of unmorality have practiced a blatant contradiction. Following in the style of [philosopher] Jean-Paul Sartre, who declared that meaningful communication is impossible even as he devoted his life to communicating meaningfully, the new moralists first proclaim that morality is capricious, perhaps even a joke, then proceed to use moral categories to condemn their opponents. These new high priests lecture us solemnly about multiculturalism, gender equality, homophobia, and environmental degradation, all the while ignoring the fact that they have systematically destroyed any basis for judging such behavior right or wrong. The emperor so quick to discourse about fashion happens to be stark naked. . . .

In a great irony, the "politically correct" movement defending the rights of women, minorities, and the environment often positions itself as an enemy of the Christian church when, in historical fact, the church has contributed the very underpinnings that make such a movement possible. Christianity brought an end to slavery, and its crusading fervor also fueled the early labor movement, women's suffrage, human-rights campaigns, and civil rights. According to [sociologist] Robert Bellah, "there has not been a major issue in the history of the United States on which religious bodies did not speak out, publicly and vociferously."

It was no accident that Christians pioneered in the antislavery movement, for their beliefs had a theological impetus. Both slavery and the oppression of women were based, anachronistically, on an embryonic form of Darwinism. Aristotle had observed that

> Tame animals are naturally better than wild animals, yet for all tame animals there is an advantage in being under human control, as this secures their survival. And as regards the relationship between male and female, the former is naturally superior, the latter inferior, the former rules and the latter is subject. By analogy, the same must necessarily apply to mankind as a whole. Therefore all men who differ from one another by as much as the soul differs from the body or man from a wild beast (and that is the state of those who work by using their bodies, and for whom that is the best they can do)—these people are slaves by nature, and it is better for them to be subject to this kind of control, as it is better for the other creatures I have mentioned. . . . It is clear that there are certain people who are free and certain people who are slaves by nature, and it is both to their advantage, and just, for them to be slaves. . . . From the hour of their birth, some men are marked out for subjection, others for rule.

Cross out the name *Aristotle* and read the paragraph again as the discovery of a leading evolutionary psychologist. No one is proposing the reimposition of slavery, of course—but why not? If we learn our morality from nature, and if our only rights are those we create for ourselves, why should not the strong exercise their "natural rights" over the weak?

The Need for a Moral Authority

As Alasdair MacIntyre remarks in *After Virtue*, modern protesters have not abandoned moral argument, though they have abandoned any coherent platform from which to make a moral argument. They keep using moral terminology—it is *wrong* to own slaves, rape a woman, abuse a child, despoil the environment, discriminate against homosexuals—but they have no "higher authority" to which to appeal to make their moral judgments. MacIntyre concludes,

> Hence the *utterance* of protest is characteristically addressed to those who already *share* the protestors' premises. The effects of incommensurability ensure that protestors rarely have anyone else to talk to but themselves. This is not to say that protest cannot be effective; it is to say that it cannot be *rationally* effective and that its dominant modes of expression give evidence of a certain perhaps unconscious awareness of this.

In the United States, we prefer to settle major issues on utilitarian or pragmatic grounds. But philosophers including Aristotle and David Hume argued powerfully in favor of slavery on those very grounds. Hitler pursued his genocidal policies against the Jews and "defective" persons on utilitarian grounds. Unless modern thinkers can locate a source of moral authority somewhere else than in the collective sentiments of human beings, we will always be vulnerable to dangerous swings of moral consensus. . . .

A Generation of Wingless Chickens

> *It is easy to see that the moral sense has been bred out of certain sections of the population, like the wings have been bred off certain chickens to produce more white meat on them. This is a generation of wingless chickens.*
>
> —Flannery O'Connor

What happens when an entire society becomes populated with wingless chickens? I need not dwell on the contemporary symptoms of moral illness in the United States: our rate of violent crime has quintupled in my lifetime; a third of all babies are now born out of wedlock; half of all marriages end in divorce; the richest nation on earth has a homeless population larger than the entire population of some nations. These familiar symptoms are just that, symptoms. A diagnosis would look beyond them to our loss of a teleological sense. "Can one be a saint if God does not exist? That is the only concrete problem I know of today," wrote Albert Camus in *The Fall*.

Butler. © 1997 by Clay Butler. Reproduced by permission.

Civilization holds together when a society learns to place moral values above the human appetites for power, wealth, violence, and pleasure. Historically, it has always relied on religion to provide a source for that moral authority. In fact, according to [historians] Will and Ariel Durant, "There is no significant example in history, before our time, of a society successfully maintaining moral life without the aid of religion." They added the foreboding remark, "The greatest question of our time is not communism versus individualism, not Europe versus America, not even the East versus the West; it is whether men can live without God."

[Playwright and former president of Czechoslovakia] Vàclav Havel, a survivor of a civilization that tried to live without God, sees the crisis clearly:

> I believe that with the loss of God, man has lost a kind of absolute and universal system of coordinates, to which he could always relate everything, chiefly himself. His world and his personality gradually began to break up into separate, incoherent fragments corresponding to different, relative, coordinates.

On moral issues—social justice, sexuality, marriage and family, definitions of life and death—society badly needs a moral tether, or "system of coordinates" in Havel's phrase. Otherwise, our laws and politics will begin to reflect the same kind of moral schizophrenia already seen in individuals.

On what moral basis do doctrinaire Darwinians, committed to the survival of the fittest, ask us to protect the environment, in effect lending a hand to those we make "unfit"? On what basis do abortionists denounce the gender-based abortion practiced in India, where, in some cities, 99 percent of abortions involve a female fetus? (For this reason, some Indian cities have made it illegal for doctors to reveal to parents a fetus's gender after an ultrasound test.) Increasingly, the schizophrenia of personal morality is being projected onto society at large.

James Davison Hunter recounts watching a segment of the *Phil Donahue Show* featuring men who left their wives and then had affairs with those wives' mothers. Some of the relationships failed, but some worked out fine, the men reported. A psychologist sitting on the panel concluded, "The important thing to remember is that there is no right or wrong. I hear no wrongdoing. As I listen to their stories, I hear pain."

The Fate of a Godless Society

Hunter speculates where a society might be headed once it loses all moral consensus. "Personally I'm into ritual animal sacrifice," says one citizen. "Oh, really," says another. "I happen to be into man-boy relationships." "That's great," responds a third, "but my preference is . . ." and so on. The logical end of such thinking, Hunter suggests, can be found in the Marquis de Sade's novel *Juliette*, which declares,

"Nothing is forbidden by nature."

In Sade's novel, Juliette's lover enhances their sexual ecstasy by raping Juliette's daughter and throwing the girl into a fire; wielding a poker, the mother herself prevents the child's escape. A brute accused of raping, sodomizing, and murdering more than two dozen boys, girls, men, and women defends himself by saying that all concepts of virtue and vice are arbitrary; self-interest is the paramount rule:

> Justice has no real existence, it is the deity of every passion.
> . . . So let us abandon our belief in this fiction, it no more exists than does the God of whom fools believe it the image; there is no God in this world, neither is there virtue, neither is there justice; there is nothing good, useful, or necessary but our passions.

U.S. courts today take pains to decide the merits of a case apart from religion or natural law. New York State passed a law prohibiting the use of children in pornographic films and, in order to protect it from civil libertarians, specified that the law is based not on moral or religious reasons, rather on "mental health" grounds. In earlier times the Supreme Court appealed to the "general consent" of society's moral values in deciding issues such as polygamy. I wonder on what possible grounds the Court might rule against polygamy today (practiced in 84 percent of all recorded cultures)—or incest, or pederasty, for that matter. All these moral taboos derive from a religious base; take away that foundation, and why should the practices be forbidden?

To ask a basic question, What sense does marriage make in a morally neutral society? A friend of mine, though gay, is nevertheless troubled by calls for gay marriages. "What's to keep two brothers from marrying, if they declare a commitment to each other?" he asks. "They could then enjoy the tax breaks and advantages of inheritance and health plans. It seems to me something more should be at stake in an institution like marriage." Yes, but *what* is at stake in marriage? The authors of *Habits of the Heart* found that few individuals in their survey except committed Christians could explain why they stayed married to their spouses. Marriage as a social construct is arbitrary, flexible, and open to redefinition. Marriage as a sacrament established by God is another matter entirely.

Separating Sex from Morality

Feminist thinkers have led the way in questioning the traditional basis of sexual ethics. In *The Erotic Silence of the American Wife*, Dalma Heyn argues that women unnaturally bind themselves at the marriage altar, abandoning their true needs and desires. Heyn recommends extramarital affairs as the cure for what she sardonically calls "the Donna Reed syndrome."[1] In an essay in *Time*, Barbara Ehrenreich celebrated the fact that "Sex can finally, after all these centuries, be separated from the all-too-serious business of reproduction. . . . The only ethic that can work in an overcrowded world is one that insists that . . . sex—preferably among affectionate and consenting adults—belongs squarely in the realm of play."

Ehrenreich and Heyn are detaching sex from any teleological meaning invested in it by religion. But why limit the experience to affectionate and consenting adults? If sex is a matter of play, why not sanction pederasty, as did the Greeks and Romans? Why choose the age of 18—or 16, or 14, or 12—to mark an arbitrary distinction between child abuse and indulging in play? If sex is mere play, why do we prosecute people for incest? (Indeed, the Sex Information and Education Council of the United States circulated a paper expressing skepticism regarding "moral and religious pronouncements with respect to incest," lamenting that the taboo has hindered scientific investigation.)

The Alice-in-Wonderland world of untethered ethics has little place for traditional morality. When California adopted a sex-education program, the American Civil Liberties Union (ACLU) sent this official memorandum:

> The ACLU regrets to inform you of our opposition to SB 2394 concerning sex education in public schools. It is our position that teaching that monogamous, heterosexual intercourse within marriage is a traditional American value is an unconstitutional establishment of religious doctrine in public schools. . . . We believe SB 2394 violates the First Amendment.

Again I stress, to me the question is not why modern secularists reject traditional morality, but on what grounds they de-

---

1. a reference to a 1960s television show featuring a traditional suburban wife and mother

fend any morality. Our legal system vigorously defends a woman's right to choose abortion—but why stop there? Historically, abandonment has been the more common means of disposing of unwanted children. Romans did it, Greeks did it, and during [philosopher Jean-Jacques] Rousseau's lifetime, one-third of babies in Paris were simply abandoned. Yet today, in the United States, if a mother leaves her baby in a Chicago alley, or two teens deposit their newborn in a Dempsey Dumpster, they are subject to prosecution.

We feel outrage when we hear of a middle-class couple "dumping" an Alzheimer's-afflicted parent when they no longer wish to care for him, or when kids push a five-year-old out the window of a high-rise building, or a ten-year-old is raped in a hallway, or a mother drowns her two children because they interfere with her lifestyle. Why? On what grounds do we feel outrage if we truly believe that morality is self-determined? Evidently the people who committed the crimes felt no compunction. And if morality is not, in the end, self-determined, who determines it? On what basis do we decide?

In the landmark book *Faith in the Future*, Jonathan Sacks, chief rabbi of the United Hebrew Congregations of the (British) Commonwealth, argues that human society was meant to be a covenant between God and humankind, a collaborative enterprise based on common values and vision. Instead, it has become "an aggregate of individuals pursuing private interest, coming together temporarily and contractually, and leaving the state to resolve their conflicts on value-neutral grounds." In the process, "the individual loses his moorings . . . and becomes prone to a sense of meaninglessness and despair." Sacks argues that only by restoring the "moral covenant" can we reverse the breakdown in the social fabric of Western civilization.

Or, as the Jewish medical educator David C. Stolinsky put it, "The reason we fear to go out after dark is not that we may be set upon by bands of evangelicals and forced to read the New Testament, but that we may be set upon by gangs of feral young people who have been taught that nothing is superior to their own needs or feelings.". . .

In his study *Morality: Religious and Secular*, Basil Mitchell argues that, since the eighteenth century, secular thinkers have attempted to make reason, not religion, the basis of morality. None has successfully found a way to establish an *absolute* value for the individual human person. Mitchell suggests that secular thinkers can establish a relative value for people, by comparing people to animals, say, or to each other; but the idea that every person has an absolute value came out of Christianity and Judaism before it and is absent from every other ancient philosophy or religion.

The Founding Fathers of the United States, apparently aware of the danger, made a valiant attempt to connect individual rights to a transcendent source. Overruling Thomas Jefferson, who had made only a vague reference to "the Laws of Nature and of Nature's God," they insisted instead on including the words "unalienable" and "endowed by their Creator." They did so in order to secure such rights in a transcendent Higher Power, so that no human power could attempt to take them away. Human dignity and worth derive from God's.

Yet if there is no Creator to endow these rights, on what basis can they be considered unalienable? Precisely that question is asked openly today. Robert Jarvik, a scientist and inventor of the artificial human heart, expresses the more modern view:

> In reality, there are no basic human rights. Mankind created them. They are conventions we agree to abide by for our mutual protection under law. Are there basic animal rights? Basic plant rights? Basic rights of any kind to protect things on our planet when the sun eventually burns out, or when we block it out with radioactive clouds? Someday, humans will realize that we are a part of nature and not separate from it. We have no more basic rights than viruses, other than those that we create for ourselves through our intellect and our compassion.

Jarvik captures the dilemma: If humans are not made in the image of God, somehow distinct from animals, what gives us any more rights than other species? Some animal rights activists already ask that question, and a writer in the journal *Wild Earth* even mused about the logical consequences:

> If you haven't given voluntary human extinction much thought before, the idea of a world with no people may seem

strange. But, if you give the idea a chance I think you might agree that the extinction of *Homo sapiens* would mean survival for millions, if not billions, of other Earth-dwelling species. . . . Phasing out the human race will solve every problem on earth, social and environmental.

When representatives from the United States meet with their counterparts from China and Singapore to hammer out an agreement on human rights, not only do they have no common ground, they have no self-coherent ground on which to stand. Our founders made human dignity an irreducible value rooted in creation, a dignity that exists prior to any "public" status as citizen. Eliminate the Creator, and everything is on the negotiating table. By destroying the link between the social and cosmic orders, we have effectively destroyed the validity of the social order.

"Our ethics can be based neither upon fictions concerning the nature of mankind nor upon fake reports concerning the desire of the deities."

Morality Does Not Require Religious Belief

Frank R. Zindler

Contrary to common belief, religion is not the foundation of morality, writes Frank R. Zindler in the following viewpoint. Moral behavior is rooted in human physiology, inherited traits, and cultural adaptations, he maintains. What we consider to be ethical conduct is actually behavior that has, over time, proved to be of benefit to individuals as well as society. According to Zindler, religion is a cultural adaptation that was useful earlier in human evolution but that should now be replaced with scientific self-knowledge. He concludes that enlightened self-interest is more appropriate than religion as a modern moral compass. Zindler, a former professor of biology and geology, is managing editor of *American Atheist* magazine.

As you read, consider the following questions:
1. What is the relationship between natural selection and morality, in Zindler's opinion?
2. According to the author, what is cultural transmission?
3. How does Zindler define "enlightened self-interest"?

Frank R. Zindler, "Ethics Without Gods," *American Atheist*, February 1985.

One of the first questions Atheists are asked by true believers and doubters alike is, "If you don't believe in a god, there's nothing to prevent you from committing crimes, is there? Without the fear of hell-fire and eternal damnation, you can do anything you like, can't you?"

It is hard to believe that even intelligent and educated people could hold such an opinion, but they do. It seems never to have occurred to them that the Greeks and Romans, whose gods and goddesses were something less than paragons of virtue, nevertheless led lives not obviously worse than those of the Baptists of Alabama. Moreover, pagans such as Aristotle and Marcus Aurelius—although their systems are not suitable for us today—managed to produce ethical treatises of great sophistication, a sophistication rarely, if ever, equaled by Christian moralists.

The answer to the question posed above is, of course, "Absolutely not!" The behavior of Atheists is subject to the same rules of sociology, psychology, and neurophysiology that govern the behavior of all members of our species, religionists included. Moreover, despite protestations to the contrary, we may assert as a general rule that when religionists practice ethical behavior, it isn't *really* due to their fear of hell-fire and damnation, or to their hopes of heaven. Ethical behavior—regardless of who the practitioner may be—results always from the same causes and is regulated by the same forces, and has nothing to do with the presence or absence of religious belief. The nature of these causes and forces is the subject of this essay.

Psychobiological Foundations

As human beings, we are social animals. Our sociality is the result of evolution, not choice. Natural selection has equipped us with nervous systems which are peculiarly sensitive to the emotional status of our fellows. Among our kind, emotions are contagious, and it is only the rare psychopathic mutants among us who can be happy in the midst of a sad society. It is in our nature to be happy in the midst of happiness, sad in the midst of sadness. It is in our nature, fortunately, to seek happiness for our fellows at the same time as we seek it for ourselves. Our happiness is greater when it is shared.

Nature also has provided us with nervous systems which are, to a considerable degree, imprintable. To be sure, this phenomenon is not as pronounced or as inelectable as it is, say, in geese—where a newly hatched gosling can be "imprinted" to a toy train and will follow it to exhaustion, as if it were its mother. Nevertheless, some degree of imprinting is exhibited by humans. The human nervous system appears to retain its capacity for imprinting well into old age, and it is highly likely that the phenomenon known as "love-at-first-sight" is a form of imprinting. Imprinting is a form of attachment behavior, and it helps us to form strong interpersonal bonds. It is a major force which helps us to break through the ego barrier to create "significant others" whom we can love as much as ourselves. These two characteristics of our nervous system—emotional suggestibility and attachment imprintability—although they are the foundation of all altruistic behavior and art, are thoroughly compatible with the selfishness characteristic of all behaviors created by the process of natural selection. That is to say, to a large extent behaviors which satisfy ourselves will be found, simultaneously, to satisfy our fellows, and *vice-versa*.

This should not surprise us when we consider that among the societies of our nearest primate cousins, the great apes, social behavior is not chaotic, even if gorillas do lack the Ten Commandments! The young chimpanzee does not need an oracle to tell it to honor its mother and to refrain from killing its brothers and sisters. Of course, family squabbles and even murder have been observed in ape societies, but such behaviors are exceptions, not the norm. So too it is in human societies, everywhere and at all times.

The African apes—whose genes are ninety-eight to ninety-nine percent identical to ours—go about their lives as social animals, cooperating in the living of life, entirely without the benefit of clergy and without the commandments of Exodus, Leviticus, or Deuteronomy. It is further cheering to learn that sociobiologists have even observed altruistic behavior among troops of baboons! More than once, in troops attacked by leopards, aged, post-reproduction-age males have been observed to linger at the rear of the escaping troop and to engage the leopard in what often amounts to a suicidal fight. As an old male delays the leopard's pursuit by sacrificing his very life, the females and young escape and live to fulfill their several destinies. The heroism which we see acted out, from time to time, by our fellow men and women, is far older than their religions. Long before the gods were created by the fear-filled minds of our less courageous ancestors, heroism and acts of self-sacrificing love existed. They did not require a supernatural excuse then, nor do they require one now.

Given the general fact, then, that evolution has equipped us with nervous systems biased in favor of social, rather than antisocial, behaviors, is it not true, nevertheless, that antisocial behavior *does* exist? And does it not exist in amounts greater than a reasonable ethicist would find tolerable? Alas, this is true. But is true largely because we live in worlds far more complex than the Paleolithic world in which our nervous systems originated. To understand the ethical significance of this fact, we must digress a bit and review the evolutionary history of human behavior.

Instinctual and Learned Behavior

Today, heredity can control our behavior in only the most general of ways; it cannot dictate precise behaviors appropriate for infinitely varied circumstances. In our world, heredity needs help.

In the world of a fruit fly, by contrast, the problems to be solved are few in number and highly predictable in nature. Consequently, a fruit fly's brain is largely "hard-wired" by heredity. That is to say, most behaviors result from environmental activation of nerve circuits which are formed automatically by the time of emergence of the adult fly. This is an extreme example of what is called instinctual behavior. Each behavior is coded for by a gene or genes which predispose the nervous system to develop certain types of circuits and not others, and it is all but impossible to act contrary to the genetically predetermined script.

The world of a mammal—say a fox—is much more complex and unpredictable than that of the fruit fly. Consequently, a fox is born with only a portion of its neuronal circuitry hardwired. Many of its neurons remain "plastic" throughout life.

That is, they may or may not hook up with each other in functional circuits, depending upon environmental circumstances. Learned behavior is behavior which results from activation of these environmentally conditioned circuits. Learning allows the individual mammal to assimilate—by trial and error—greater numbers of adaptive behaviors than could be transmitted by heredity. A fox would be wall-to-wall genes if all its behaviors were specified genetically!

Morality Does Not Depend on Faith

Plato argued that the chariot of the soul is led by three horses—passion, ambition, and reason—and he thought that the rational person under the control of wisdom could lead a noble life of balance and moderation. The goal is to realize our creative potentialities to the fullest, and this includes our capacity for moral behavior. A good life is achievable by men and women without the need for divinity. It is simply untrue that if one does not believe in God, "anything goes."

So many infamous deeds have been perpetrated in the name of God—the Crusades, the Inquisition, religious-inspired terrorism . . . that it is difficult to blithely maintain that belief in God guarantees morality. It is thus the height of intolerance to insist that only those who accept religious dogma are moral, and that those who do not are wicked.

Paul Kurtz, *Free Inquiry*, Spring 1996.

With the evolution of humans, however, environmental complexity increased out of all proportion to the genetic and neuronal changes distinguishing us from our simian ancestors. This was due partly to the fact that our species evolved in a geologic period of great climatic flux—the Ice Ages—and partly to the fact that our behaviors themselves began to change our environment. The changed environment in turn created new problems to be solved. Their solutions further changed the environment, and so on. Thus, the discovery of fire led to the burning of trees and forests, which led to destruction of local water supplies and watersheds, which led to the development of architecture with which to build aqueducts, which led to laws concerning water rights, which led to international strife, and on and on.

Given such complexity, even the ability to learn new behaviors is, by itself, inadequate. If trial and error were the only means, most people would die of old age before they would succeed in rediscovering fire or reinventing the wheel. As a substitute for instinct and to increase the efficiency of learning, mankind developed culture. The ability to teach—as well as to learn—evolved, and trial-and-error learning became a method of last resort.

By transmission of culture—passing on the sum total of the learned behaviors common to a population—we can do what Darwinian genetic selection would not allow: we can inherit acquired characteristics. The wheel once having been invented, its manufacture and use can be passed down through generations. Culture can adapt to change much faster than genes can, and this provides for finely tuned responses to environmental disturbances and upheavals. By means of cultural transmission, those behaviors which have proven useful in the past can be taught quickly to the young, so that adaptation to life—say on the Greenland ice cap— can be assured.

Even so, cultural transmission tends to be rigid: it took over one hundred thousand years to advance to chipping *both* sides of the hand ax! Cultural mutations, like genetic mutations, tend more often than not to be harmful, and both are resisted—the former by cultural conservatism, the latter by natural selection. But changes do creep in faster than the rate of genetic change, and cultures slowly evolve. Even that cultural dinosaur known as the Roman Catholic church— despite its claim to be the unchanging repository of truth and correct behavior—has changed greatly since its beginning.

Incidentally, it is this hand ax stage of behavioral evolution at which most of the religions of today are still stuck. Our inflexible, absolutist moral codes also are fixated at this stage. The Ten Commandments are the moral counterpart of the "here's-how-you-rub-the-sticks-together" phase of technological evolution. If the only type of fire you want is one to heat your cave and cook your clams, the stick-rubbing method suffices. But if you want a fire to propel your jet airplane, some changes have to be made.

So, too, with the transmission of moral behavior. If we are to live lives which are as complex socially as jet airplanes are complex technologically, we need something more than the Ten Commandments. We cannot base our moral code upon arbitrary and capricious fiats reported to us by persons claiming to be privy to the intentions of the denizens of Sinai or Olympus. Our ethics can be based neither upon fictions concerning the nature of mankind nor upon fake reports concerning the desire of the deities. Our ethics must be firmly planted in the soil of scientific self-knowledge. They must be *improvable* and *adaptable*.

Where then, and with what, shall we begin?

The Principle of Enlightened Self-Interest

The principle of "enlightened self-interest" is an excellent first approximation to an ethical principle which is both consistent with what we know of human nature and is relevant to the problems of life in a complex society. Let us examine this principle.

First we must distinguish between "enlightened" and "unenlightened" self-interest. Let's take an extreme example for illustration. Suppose a person lived a totally selfish life of immediate gratification of every desire. Suppose that whenever someone else had something he wanted, he took it for himself.

It wouldn't be long at all before everyone would be up in arms against him, and he would have to spend all his waking hours fending off reprisals. Depending upon how outrageous his activity had been, he might very well lose his life in an orgy of neighborly revenge. The life of total but unenlightened self-interest might be exciting and pleasant as long as it lasts—but it is not likely to last long.

The person who practices "enlightened" self-interest, by contrast, is the person whose behavioral strategy simultaneously maximizes both the *intensity* and *duration* of personal gratification. An enlightened strategy will be one which, when practiced over a long span of time, will generate ever greater amounts and varieties of pleasures and satisfactions.

How is this to be done?

It is obvious that more is to be gained by cooperating with others than by acts of isolated egoism. One man with a rock cannot kill a buffalo for dinner. But a group of men or women, with a lot of rocks, can drive the beast off a cliff and—even after dividing the meat up among them—will still have more to eat than they would have had without cooperation.

Cooperation

But cooperation is a two-way street. If you cooperate with several others to kill buffalo, and each time they drive you away from the kill and eat it themselves, you will quickly take your services elsewhere, and you will leave the ingrates to stumble along without the Paleolithic equivalent of a fourth-for-bridge. Cooperation implies reciprocity.

Justice has its roots in the problem of determining fairness and reciprocity in cooperation. If I cooperate with you in tilling your field of corn, how much of the corn is due me at harvest time? When there is justice, cooperation operates at maximal efficiency, and the fruits of cooperation become ever more desirable. Thus, "enlightened self-interest" entails a desire for justice. With justice and with cooperation, we can have symphonies. Without it, we haven't even a song.

Because we have the nervous systems of social animals, we are generally happier in the company of our fellow creatures than alone. Because we are emotionally suggestible, as we practice enlightened self-interest, we usually will be wise to choose behaviors which will make others happy and willing to cooperate and accept us—for their happiness will reflect back upon us and intensify our own happiness. On the other hand, actions which harm others and make them unhappy— even if they do not trigger overt retaliation which decreases our happiness—will create an emotional milieu which, because of our suggestibility, will make us less happy.

Because our nervous systems are imprintable, we are able not only to fall in love at first sight, we are able to love objects and ideals as well as people. We are also able to love with variable intensities. Like the gosling attracted to the toy train, we are pulled forward by the desire for love. Unlike the gosling's "love," however, our love is to a considerable extent shapable by experience and is educable. A major aim of "enlightened self-interest," surely, is to give and receive love, both sexual and non-sexual. As a general—though not absolute—rule, we must choose those behaviors which will be likely to bring us love and acceptance, and we must eschew those behaviors which will not.

Another aim of enlightened self-interest is to seek beauty in all its forms, to preserve and prolong its resonance between the world outside and that within. Beauty and love are but different facets of the same jewel: Love is beautiful, and we love beauty.

The experience of love and beauty, however, is a *passive* function of the mind. How much greater is the joy which comes from creating beauty! How delicious it is to exercise *actively* our creative powers to engender that which can be loved! Paints and pianos are not necessarily prerequisites for the exercise of creativity: Whenever one transforms the raw materials of existence in such a way that he leaves them better than they were when he found them, he has been creative.

The Task of Moral Education

The task of moral education, then, is not to inculcate by rote great lists of do's and don'ts but rather to help people to predict the consequences of actions being considered. What are the long-term and immediate rewards and drawbacks of the acts? Will an act increase or decrease one's chances of experiencing the hedonic triad of love, beauty, and creativity?

Thus it happens, that when the Atheist approaches the problem of finding natural grounds for human morals and establishing a non-superstitious basis for behavior, it appears as though nature has already solved the problem to a great extent. Indeed, it appears as though the problem of establishing a natural, humanistic basis for ethical behavior is not much of a problem at all. It is in our natures to desire love, to seek beauty, and to thrill at the act of creation. The labyrinthine complexity we see when we examine traditional moral codes does not arise of necessity: It is largely the result of vain attempts to accommodate human needs and nature to the whimsical totems and taboos of the demons and deities who emerged with us from our cave dwellings at the end of the Paleolithic Era—and have haunted our houses ever since.

*"[Secular humanists] wish to encourage
wherever possible the growth of moral
awareness and the capacity for free choice."*

Secular Humanism Encourages
Moral Awareness

Paul Kurtz

Paul Kurtz is founder and chair of the Council for Secular
Humanism and president of the International Academy of
Humanism. He is also editor in chief of *Free Inquiry*, a quar-
terly journal of humanist thought. In the following viewpoint
Kurtz defines some of the principles of secular humanism, a
worldview that upholds reason, freedom, and human rights
while opposing religious belief and superstition. Kurtz maintains that secular humanism has greatly contributed to the
development of a more humane and democratic world. By
promoting freedom of thought, church-state separation, and
systems of ethics informed by reason, secular humanism provides a way for people to articulate moral principles.

As you read, consider the following questions:
1. What antisecularist trends does the world face today, in
   Kurtz's opinion?
2. According to the author, who are some secularists and
   humanists who have demonstrated morality in their lives
   and works?
3. According to Kurtz, why do secularists believe it is
   immoral to baptize infants or confirm adolescents?

S ecular humanism is a vital force in the contemporary world. It is now under unwarranted and intemperate attack from various quarters. This declaration defends only that form of secular humanism which is explicitly committed to democracy. It is opposed to all varieties of belief that seek supernatural sanction for their values or espouse rule by dictatorship.

Democratic secular humanism has been a powerful force in world culture. Its ideals can be traced to the philosophers, scientists, and poets of classical Greece and Rome, to ancient Chinese Confucian society, to the Carvaka movement of India, and to other distinguished intellectual and moral traditions. Secularism and humanism were eclipsed in Europe during the Dark Ages, when religious piety eroded humankind's confidence in its own powers to solve human problems. They reappeared in force during the Renaissance with the reassertion of secular and humanist values in literature and the arts, again in the sixteenth and seventeenth centuries with the development of modern science and a naturalistic view of the universe, and their influence can be found in the eighteenth century in the Age of Reason and the Enlightenment.

Democratic secular humanism has creatively flowered in modern times with the growth of freedom and democracy. Countless millions of thoughtful persons have espoused secular humanist ideals, have lived significant lives, and have contributed to the building of a more humane and democratic world. The modern secular humanist outlook has led to the application of science and technology to the improvement of the human condition. This has had a positive effect on reducing poverty, suffering, and disease in various parts of the world, in extending longevity, on improving transportation and communication, and in making the good life possible for more and more people. It has led to the emancipation of hundreds of millions of people from the exercise of blind faith and fears of superstition and has contributed to their education and the enrichment of their lives.

Antisecularist Trends

Secular humanism has provided an impetus for humans to solve their problems with intelligence and perseverance, to conquer geographic and social frontiers, and to extend the range of human exploration and adventure. Regrettably, we are today faced with a variety of antisecularist trends: the reappearance of dogmatic authoritarian religions; fundamentalist, literalist, and doctrinaire Christianity; a rapidly growing and uncompromising Moslem clericalism in the Middle East and Asia; the reassertion of orthodox authority by the Roman Catholic papal hierarchy; nationalistic religious Judaism, and the reversion to obscurantist religions in Asia.

New cults of unreason as well as bizarre paranormal and occult beliefs, such as belief in astrology, reincarnation, and the mysterious power of alleged psychics, are growing in many Western societies. These disturbing developments follow in the wake of the emergence in the earlier part of the twentieth century of intolerant messianic and totalitarian quasi religious movements, such as fascism and communism. These religious activists not only are responsible for much of the terror and violence in the world today but stand in the way of solutions to the world's most serious problems.

Paradoxically, some of the critics of secular humanism maintain that it is a dangerous philosophy. Some assert that it is "morally corrupting" because it is committed to individual freedom, others that it condones "injustice" because it defends democratic due process. We who support democratic secular humanism deny such charges, which are based upon misunderstanding and misinterpretation, and we seek to outline a set of principles that most of us share.

Secular humanism is not a dogma or a creed. There are wide differences of opinion among secular humanists on many issues. Nevertheless, there is a loose consensus with respect to several propositions. We are apprehensive that modern civilization is threatened by forces antithetical to reason, democracy, and freedom. Many religious believers will no doubt share with us a belief in many secular humanist and democratic values, and we welcome their joining with us in the defense of these ideals.

Free Inquiry

The first principle of democratic secular humanism is its commitment to free inquiry. We oppose any tyranny over the mind of man, any efforts by ecclesiastical, political, ideological, or social institutions to shackle free thought. In the past, such tyrannies have been directed by churches and states attempting to enforce the edicts of religious bigots. In the long struggle in the history of ideas, established institutions, both public and private, have attempted to censor inquiry, to impose orthodoxy on beliefs and values, and to excommunicate heretics and extirpate unbelievers. Today, the struggle for free inquiry has assumed new forms. Sectarian ideologies have become the new theologies that use political parties and governments in their mission to crush dissident opinion. Free inquiry entails recognition of civil liberties as integral to its pursuit, that is, a free press, freedom of communication, the right to organize opposition parties and to join voluntary associations, and freedom to cultivate and publish the fruits of scientific, philosophical, artistic, literary, moral and religious freedom. Free inquiry requires that we tolerate diversity of opinion and that we respect the right of individuals to express their beliefs, however unpopular they may be, without social or legal prohibition or fear of sanctions. Though we may tolerate contrasting points of view, this does not mean that they are immune to critical scrutiny. The guiding premise of those who believe in free inquiry is that truth is more likely to be discovered if the opportunity exists for the free exchange of opposing opinions; the process of interchange is frequently as important as the result. This applies not only to science and to everyday life, but to politics, economics, morality, and religion.

Separation of Church and State

Because of their commitment to freedom, secular humanists believe in the principle of the separation of church and state. The lessons of history are clear: wherever one religion or ideology is established and given a dominant position in the state, minority opinions are in jeopardy. A pluralistic, open, democratic society allows all points of view to be heard. Any effort to impose an exclusive conception of Truth, Piety, Virtue, or Justice upon the whole of society is a violation of free inquiry. Clerical authorities should not be permitted to legislate their own parochial views—whether moral, philosophical, political, educational, or social—for the rest of society. Nor should tax revenues be exacted for the benefit or support of sectarian religious institutions. Individuals and voluntary associations should be free to accept or not to accept any belief and to support these convictions with whatever resources they may have, without being compelled by taxation to contribute to those religious faiths with which they do not agree. . . .

Ethics Based on Critical Intelligence

The moral views of secular humanism have been subjected to criticism by religious fundamentalist theists. The secular humanist recognizes the central role of morality in human life; indeed, ethics was developed as a branch of human knowledge long before religionists proclaimed their moral systems based upon divine authority. The field of ethics has had a distinguished list of thinkers contributing to its development: from Socrates, Democritus, Aristotle, Epicurus, and Epictetus, to Spinoza, Erasmus, Hume, Voltaire, Kant, Bentham, Mill, G.E. Moore, Bertrand Russell, John Dewey, and others. There is an influential philosophical tradition that maintains that ethics is an autonomous field of inquiry, that ethical judgments can be formulated independently of revealed religion, and that human beings can cultivate practical reason and wisdom and, by its application, achieve lives of virtue and excellence. Moreover, philosophers have emphasized the need to cultivate an appreciation for the requirements of social justice and for an individual's obligations and responsibilities toward others. Thus, secularists deny that morality needs to be deduced from religious belief or that those who do not espouse a religious doctrine are immoral. For secular humanists, ethical conduct is, or should be, judged by critical reason, and their goal is to develop autonomous and responsible individuals, capable of making their own choices in life based upon an understanding of human behavior. Morality that is not God-based need not be antisocial, subjective, or promiscuous, nor need it lead to the breakdown of moral standards. Although we believe in tolerating diverse lifestyles and social manners, we do not think they are immune to criticism. Nor do we believe that any one church should impose its views of moral virtue and sin, sexual conduct, marriage, divorce, birth

What the Humanist Believes

Humanism is opposed to all theories of universal determinism, fatalism, or predestination and believes that human beings possess genuine freedom of choice (free will) in making decisions both important and unimportant. Free choice is conditioned by inheritance, education, the external environment (including economic conditions), and other factors. Nonetheless, it remains real and substantial. Humanism rejects both Marxist economic determinism and Christian theistic determinism.

Humanism advocates an ethics or morality that grounds all human values in this-earthly experiences and relationships, and that views man as a functioning unity of physical, emotional, and intellectual faculties. The Humanist holds as his highest ethical goal the this-worldly happiness, freedom, and progress—economic, cultural, and material—of all mankind, irrespective of nation, race, religion, sex, or economic status. Reserving the word *love* for their families and friends, he has an attitude of *compassionate concern* toward his fellow men in general.

Corliss Lamont, *Humanist*, September/October 1971.

control, or abortion, or legislate them for the rest of society. As secular humanists we believe in the central importance of the value of human happiness here and now. We are opposed to absolutist morality, yet we maintain that objective standards emerge, and ethical values and principles may be discovered, in the course of ethical deliberation. Secular humanist ethics maintains that it is possible for human beings to lead meaningful and wholesome lives for themselves and in service to their fellow human beings without the need of religious commandments or the benefit of clergy. There have been any number of distinguished secularists and humanists who have demonstrated moral principles in their personal lives and works: Protagoras, Lucretius, Epicurus, Spinoza, Hume, Thomas Paine, Diderot, Mark Twain, George Eliot, John Stuart Mill, Ernest Renan, Charles Darwin, Thomas Edison, Clarence Darrow, Robert Ingersoll, Gilbert Murray, Albert Schweitzer, Albert Einstein, Max Born, Margaret Sanger, and Bertrand Russell, among others.

We believe that moral development should be cultivated in children and young adults. We do not believe that any particular sect can claim important values as their exclusive property; hence it is the duty of public education to deal with these values. Accordingly, we support moral education in the schools that is designed to develop an appreciation for moral virtues, intelligence, and the building of character. We wish to encourage wherever possible the growth of moral awareness and the capacity for free choice and an understanding of the consequences thereof. We do not think it is moral to baptize infants, to confirm adolescents, or to impose a religious creed on young people before they are able to consent. Although children should learn about the history of religious moral practices, these young minds should not be indoctrinated in a faith before they are mature enough to evaluate the merits for themselves. It should be noted that secular humanism is not so much a specific morality as it is a method for the explanation and discovery of rational moral principles. . . .

Religious Skepticism

Religions are pervasive sociological phenomena, and religious myths have long persisted in human history. In spite of the fact that human beings have found religions to be uplifting and a source of solace, we do not find their theological claims to be true. Religions have made negative as well as positive contributions toward the development of human civilization. Although they have helped to build hospitals and schools and, at their best, have encouraged the spirit of love and charity, many have also caused human suffering by being intolerant of those who did not accept their dogmas or creeds. Some religions have been fanatical and repressive, narrowing human hopes, limiting aspirations, and precipitating religious wars and violence. While religions have no doubt offered comfort to the bereaved and dying by holding forth the promise of an immortal life, they have also aroused morbid fear and dread. We have found no convincing evidence that there is a separable "soul" or that it exists before birth or survives death. We must therefore conclude that the ethical life can be lived without the illusions of immortality or reincarnation. Human beings can develop the self confidence necessary to ameliorate the human condition and to lead meaningful, productive lives. . . .

Approaching the Human Situation Realistically

Democratic secular humanism is too important for human civilization to abandon. Reasonable persons will surely recognize its profound contributions to human welfare. We are nevertheless surrounded by doomsday prophets of disaster, always wishing to turn the clock back—they are anti science, anti freedom, anti human. In contrast, the secular humanistic outlook is basically melioristic, looking forward with hope rather than backward with despair. We are committed to extending the ideals of reason, freedom, individual and collective opportunity, and democracy throughout the world community. The problems that humankind will face in the future, as in the past, will no doubt be complex and difficult. However, if it is to prevail, it can only do so by enlisting resourcefulness and courage. Secular humanism places trust in human intelligence rather than in divine guidance. Skeptical of theories of redemption, damnation, and reincarnation, secular humanists attempt to approach the human situation in realistic terms: human beings are responsible for their own destinies. We believe that it is possible to bring about a more humane world, one based upon the methods of reason and the principles of tolerance, compromise, and the negotiations of difference.

"Secular societies believe they have left religion behind, when all they have done is substitute one set of myths for another."

Secular Humanism Is Harmful

John Gray

In the following viewpoint John Gray argues that secular humanism is harmful because it suppresses natural human inclinations and fosters tyranny in the name of progress and science. Liberal humanism is actually a secular cult that developed out of Christianity's separation of religion and politics. In effect, Gray explains, secular humanism is a belief system that tries to deny its own religious roots. What secularists fail to recognize is that religious belief is a natural human impulse, Gray contends. When secular societies attempt to deny religion, the repressed religious instinct eventually reasserts itself in bizarre and dangerous ways. The author of many books on political theory, Gray is a professor of European thought at the London School of Economics in England.

As you read, consider the following questions:
1. According to Gray, what is the biblical root of the secular state?
2. What is positivism, according to the author?
3. In what way are Christian myths more realistic than secular doctrines, in Gray's opinion?

John Gray, "The Myth of Secularism: Religion Is a Natural Human Impulse, Which Our Society Tries to Repress Just as the Victorians Did Sex. That Is Why Atheists Are So Rancorous and Intolerant," *New Statesman*, vol. 131, December 16, 2002, pp. 69–71. Copyright © 2002 by New Statesman, Ltd. Reproduced by permission.

Of all the myths spawned by the Enlightenment, the idea that we live in a secular age is the most absurd. Throughout much of the world, religion is thriving with undiminished vitality. Where believers are in the minority, as they are in Britain today, traditional faiths have been replaced by liberal humanism, which is now established as the unthinking creed of conventional people. Yet liberal humanism is itself very obviously a religion—a shoddy derivative of Christian faith notably more irrational than the original article, and in recent times more harmful. If this is not recognised, it is because religion has been repressed from consciousness in the way that sexuality was repressed in Victorian times. Now as then, the result is not that the need disappears, but rather that it returns in bizarre and perverse forms. Secular societies may imagine they are post-religious, but actually they are ruled by repressed religion.

When thinking about the idea that we live in a post-religious era, it is worth remembering that the secular realm is a Christian invention. The biblical root of the secular state is the passage in the New Testament where Jesus tells his disciples to give to God what is God's and to Caesar what belongs to Caesar. Refined by Augustine and given a modern formulation with the Reformation, this early Christian commandment is the ultimate origin of the liberal attempt to separate religion from politics. In this, as in many other respects, liberalism is a neo-Christian cult.

Liberalism's Religious Roots

Liberalism's religious roots are opaque to liberals today, but a little history makes them clear. In Britain, until the late 19th century, most liberals were believers. It was churchmen who most consistently upheld causes such as the abolition of slavery; the more radical thinkers belonged to fringe Christian denominations such as the Quakers and the Unitarians. Only with John Stuart Mill, when he came under the influence of the French positivist thinker Auguste Comte, did liberalism come to be closely associated with outright rejection of conventional religion. Positivism is largely forgotten today, and not without good reason. Nevertheless, it was more influential than any other intellectual movement in shaping the humanist creed that has succeeded Christianity as the ready-made world-view of the British majority. The positivists were not liberals—far from it. They aimed to found a new religion—the Religion of Humanity, as they called it—in which the human species would be worshipped as the supreme being, and they looked forward to a time when this new religion would have as much power as the Catholic Church had in mediaeval times. They were eager to emulate the Church's rituals and hierarchies. They sought to replace the Catholic practice of crossing oneself by a secular version, in which positivist believers touched the bumps on their heads at the points where the science of phrenology had shown the impulses of order and benevolence to reside. They also installed a secular pope in Paris. In its early 19th-century heyday, the Positivist Church had Temples of Humanity in many parts of the world, including Britain. It was particularly successful in Latin America, where a number of positivist churches survive to this day.

The Positivist Church was a travesty, but its beliefs chimed with many of Mill's. Though he attacked Comte's anti-liberal tendencies, Mill did everything he could to propagate the Religion of Humanity. If he had some success, the reason was chiefly that the new humanist religion had a great deal in common with the creed it was meant to supplant. Liberal humanism inherits several key Christian beliefs—above all, the belief that humans are categorically different from all other animals. According to humanists, humans are unique in that, using the power over nature given them by science, they can create a world better than any that has existed before. In this view, the earth is simply a mass of resources for human use, and the other animals with which we share it have no value in themselves. Those who hold to this view of things see themselves as tough-minded scientific realists, but in fact they are in the grip of one of the worst legacies of Christianity. The humanist view of the earth as an instrument of human purpose is a secular rendition of the biblical myth of Genesis. . . .

The Trouble with Secular Myths

The role of hollowed-out versions of Christian myth in humanist thought is particularly clear in the case of Marxism.

Marx's absurd idea of "the end of history", in which communism triumphs and destructive conflict then vanishes from the world, is transparently a secular mutation of Christian apocalyptic beliefs. The same is true of Francis Fukuyama's equally preposterous belief in universal salvation through "global democratic capitalism". In both cases, what we have is myth masquerading as science.

A Basic Need

Most of the people I met in intellectual, academic, or liberal circles seemed to feel that religion and spirituality were for people who were culturally or intellectually retarded, for people who couldn't handle the world and hence "needed that sort of thing." The very idea of "needing" was seen as a sign of being weak, undeveloped, retarded, because, of course, people who are cool can stand alone without "need" of anything or anyone. It was these "ordinary people," I was taught, who were such jerks that they . . . clung to religion and spirituality because thinking in a clear and rational way was beyond their capacities and scared them too much. . . .

But what I discovered was something quite different, namely, that [ordinary people] . . . were just as concerned with meaning as anyone else, including any of us who consider ourselves intellectual or agents of social change.

Connection to Spirit is as essential as oxygen. It's a basic need.

Yet, we have taught ourselves to see people as a bunch of isolated machines driven by the need for food, sex, and power. We have acted as though we could cut ourselves off from our Divine essence as manifestations of Spirit. We have built social and economic institutions and have raised children as though we did not know that we are part of the spiritual order of the universe and that our hunger for spiritual connection is every bit as urgent as our hunger for food.

Michael Lerner, *Spirit Matters*, 2000.

The trouble with secular myths is that they are frequently more harmful than the real thing. In traditional Christianity, the apocalyptic impulse was restrained by the insight that human beings are ineradicably flawed. In the secular religions that flowed from Christianity, this insight was lost. The result has been a form of tyranny, new in history, that commits vast crimes in the pursuit of heaven on earth.

Atheist Regimes

The role of humanist thought in shaping the past century's worst regimes is easily demonstrable, but it is passed over, or denied, by those who harp on about the crimes of religion. Yet the mass murders of the 20th century were not perpetrated by some latter-day version of the Spanish Inquisition. They were done by atheist regimes in the service of Enlightenment ideals of progress. Stalin and Mao were not believers in original sin. Even Hitler, who despised Enlightenment values of equality and freedom, shared the Enlightenment faith that a new world could be created by human will. Each of these tyrants imagined that the human condition could be transformed through the use of science.

History has demolished these ambitions. Even so, they have not been abandoned. In dilute and timorous forms, they continue to animate liberal humanists. Humanists angrily deny harbouring the vast hopes of Marx or Comte, but still insist that the growth of scientific knowledge enables mankind to construct a future better than anything in the past. There is not the slightest scientific warrant for this belief. It is faith, pure and simple. More, it is Christian faith—the myth that, unlike other animals, "we" can shape the future.

The irony of secular cultures is that they are ruled by myths. It is a commonplace that science has displaced religion. What is less often noted is that science has become a vehicle for needs that are indisputably religious. Like religion in the past, though less effectively, science offers meaning and hope. In politics, improvement is fragmentary and reversible. In science, the growth of knowledge is cumulative and now seemingly unstoppable. Science gives a sensation of progress that politics cannot deliver. It is an illusion, but that in no way diminishes its power. We may live in a post-Christian culture, but the idea of providence has not disappeared. People still need to believe that a benign pattern can be glimpsed in the chaos of human events.

The Repression of Religious Experience

The need for religion appears to be hard-wired in the human animal. Certainly the behaviour of secular humanists supports this hypothesis. Atheists are usually just as emotionally

174

engaged as believers. Quite commonly, they are more intellectually rigid. One cannot engage in dialogue with religious thinkers in Britain today without quickly discovering that they are, on the whole, more intelligent, better educated and strikingly more freethinking than unbelievers (as evangelical atheists still incongruously describe themselves). No doubt there are many reasons for this state of affairs, but I suspect it is the repression of the religious impulse that explains the obsessive rigidity of secular thought.

Liberal humanists repress religious experience—in themselves and others—in much the way that sexuality was repressed in the strait-laced societies of the past. When I refer to repression here, I mean it in precisely the Freudian sense. In secular cultures, religion is buried in the unconscious, only to reappear—as sex did among the Victorians—in grotesque and illicit forms. If, as some claim, the Victorians covered piano legs in a vain effort to exorcise sex from their lives, secular humanists behave similarly when they condemn religion as irrational. It seems not to have occurred to them to ask where it comes from. History and anthropology show it to be a species-wide phenomenon. There is no more reason to think that we will cease to be religious animals than there is to think we will some day be asexual.

Whatever their disciples may say today, Karl Marx and John Stuart Mill were adamant that religion would die out with the advance of science. That has not come about, and there is not the remotest prospect of it happening in the foreseeable future. Yet the idea that religion can be eradicated from human life remains an anxiously defended article of faith among secular humanists. As secular ideology is dumped throughout the world, they are left disoriented and gawping.

It is this painful cognitive dissonance, I believe, that accounts for the peculiar rancour and intolerance of many secular thinkers. Unable to account for the irrepressible vitality of religion, they can react only with puritanical horror and stigmatise it as irrational. Yet the truth is that if religion is irrational, so is the human animal. As is shown by the behaviour of humanists, this is never more so than when it imagines itself to be ruled by reason. . . .

The Paradox of Secularism

Here we have the paradox of secularism. Secular societies believe they have left religion behind, when all they have done is substitute one set of myths for another. It is far from clear that this amounts to an improvement. Christian myth has harmful aspects, not least its ingrained anthropocentrism. Even so, in insisting that human nature is incorrigibly flawed it is far more realistic than the secular doctrines that followed it. In effect, liberal humanism has taken Christianity's unhappiest myth—the separation of humans from the rest of the natural world—and stripped it of the transcendental content that gave it meaning. In so doing, it has left secular cultures such as Britain stuck between a humanist view of mankind that actually comes from religion and a more genuinely scientific view in which it is just one animal species, no more capable of taking charge of its destiny than any other. . . .

Humanism is not an alternative to religious belief, but rather a degenerate and unwitting version of it. Among the many varieties of religious life that are thriving among us—Hindu and Buddhist, Jewish and Muslim, along with many new and hybrid traditions—this pale shadow of Christianity is surely an anomaly.

Weighed down with fears and anxieties that the rest of us have never known or have long since left behind, it survives only as a remnant of a time when religion suppressed natural human impulses. We may not be far from a time when atheism will be seen as a relic of repression, like the frills that may once have been draped over piano legs.

| *"There is good evidence for the existence of genuine altruism."*

Altruism Promotes Moral Behavior

Alfie Kohn

Alfie Kohn speaks and writes widely on human behavior, education, and parenting. He is the author of *Punished by Rewards* and *No Contest: The Case Against Competition*. In the viewpoint that follows, Kohn maintains that helpful behavior is primarily motivated by altruism. While many philosophers and psychologists have argued that people generally act out of self-interest—even when they are apparently helping others—recent research suggests that those who voluntarily help are generally not seeking to impress others or ease their own feelings of distress. Instead, Kohn asserts, they are acting out of empathy—the ability to feel other people's pain and to understand other people's perspectives.

As you read, consider the following questions:
1. What kind of people are the most likely to assist others, according to Kohn?
2. What experiments have been conducted to define what motivates people to help others, according to the author?
3. In Kohn's view, how does culture influence our motivation to care about others?

You realize you left your wallet on the bus and you give up hope of ever seeing it again. But someone calls that evening asking how to return the wallet to you.

Two toddlers are roughhousing when one suddenly begins to cry. The other child rushes to fetch his own security blanket and offers it to his playmate.

Driving on a lonely country road, you see a car stopped on the shoulder, smoke pouring from the hood. The driver waves to you frantically, and instinctively you pull over to help, putting aside thoughts of your appointments.

Prosocial Behavior

Despite the fact that "Look out for Number One" is one of our culture's mantras, these examples of "prosocial" behavior are really not so unusual. "Even in our society," says New York University psychologist Martin Hoffman, "the evidence is overwhelming that most people, when confronted with someone in a distress situation, will make a move to help very quickly if circumstances permit."

Helping may be as dramatic as agreeing to donate a kidney or as mundane as letting another shopper ahead of you in line. But most of us do it frequently and started doing it very early in life.

Psychologists have argued for years about whether our behavior owes more to the situations in which we find ourselves or to our individual characteristics. Prosocial behavior seems to be related to both. On the situation side, research shows that regardless of your personality, you'll be more likely to come to someone's aid if that person is already known to you or is seen as similar to you. Likewise, if you live in a small town rather than a city, the chances of your agreeing to help increase dramatically. In one experiment, a child stood on a busy street and said to passersby, "I'm lost. Can you call my house?" Nearly three-quarters of the adults in small towns did so, as compared with fewer than half in big cities. "City people adjust to the constant demands of urban life by reducing their involvement with others," the researcher concluded. You are also more likely to help someone if no one else is around at the time you hear a cry for help. The original research on this question was conducted by psychologists Bibb Latane and John Darley. They offer three reasons to account for the fact that we're less apt to help when more people are in the area: First, we may get a case of stage fright, fearing to appear foolish if it turns out no help was really necessary. Second, we may conclude from the fact that other people aren't helping that there's really no need for us to intervene either. Finally, the responsibility for doing something is shared by everyone present, so we don't feel a personal obligation to get involved.

But some people seem to be more other-oriented than others regardless of the situation. People who feel in control of what happens in their lives and who have little need for approval from others are the most likely to help others. Similarly, people in a good state of mind, even if only temporarily, are especially inclined to help. "Feel good, do good" is the general rule, researchers say, regardless of whether you feel good from having had a productive day at the office or, say, from finding money in the street. In one study, people got a phone call from a woman who said the operator had given her their number by mistake, and she was now out of change at a pay phone. The woman asked if the person who answered would look up a number, call and deliver a message for her. It turned out that people who had unexpectedly received free stationery a few minutes before were more likely to help out the caller.

Motives for Helping Others

But some investigators aren't satisfied with knowing just when prosocial acts will take place or by whom. "Why should we help other people? Why not help Number One? That's the rock-bottom question," says University of Massachusetts psychologist Ervin Staub, who's been wrestling with that problem since the mid 1960s.

Obviously we do help each other. But it's equally obvious that our motives for doing so aren't always unselfish. Prosocial behavior, which means behavior intended to benefit others, isn't necessarily altruistic. The 17th-century political philosopher Thomas Hobbes, who believed that we always act out of self-interest, was once seen giving money to a beggar. When asked why, he explained that he was mostly trying to relieve his own distress at seeing the beggar's distress.

His explanation will ring true for many of us. But is this always what's going on: helping in order to feel good or to benefit ourselves in some way? Is real altruism a Sunday school myth? Many of us automatically assume so—not because there's good evidence for that belief but because of our basic, and unproved, assumptions about human nature.

Evidence of Genuine Altruism

New research describes how we feel when helping someone, but that doesn't mean we came to that person's aid in order to feel good. We may have acted out of a simple desire to help. In fact, there is good evidence for the existence of genuine altruism. Consider:

• Do we help just to impress others? "If looking good were the motive, you'd be more likely to help with others watching," says Latane. His experiments showed just the opposite. More evidence comes from an experiment Staub did in 1970: Children who voluntarily shared their candy turned out to have a lower need for approval than those who didn't share. "If I'm feeling good about myself, I can respond to the needs of others," Staub explains. So helping needn't be motivated by a desire for approval.

• Do we help just to ease our own distress? Sometimes our motivation is undoubtedly like that of Hobbes. But the easiest way to stop feeling bad about someone else's suffering is "just to ignore it or leave," says Arizona State University psychologist Nancy Eisenberg. Instead we often stay and help, and "there's no reason to believe we do that just to make ourselves feel better."

When people are distressed over another person's pain they may help—for selfish reasons. But if they have the chance simply to turn away from the cause of their distress, they'll gladly do that instead. People who choose to help when they have the opportunity to pass by, like the biblical Good Samaritan, aren't motivated by their own discomfort. And these people, according to C. Daniel Batson, a psychologist at the University of Kansas, describe their feelings as compassionate and sympathetic rather than anxious and apprehensive.

Batson explored this behavior by having students listen to a radio news broadcast about a college senior whose parents had just been killed in a car accident. The students who responded most empathically to her problem also offered the most help, even though it would have been easy for them to say no and put the whole thing out of their minds.

• Do we help just to feel pleased with ourselves or to avoid guilt? The obvious way to test this, Batson argues, is to see how we feel after learning that "someone else" has come to a victim's aid. If we really cared only about patting ourselves on the back (or escaping twinges of guilt), we would insist on being the rescuer. But sometimes we are concerned only to make sure that the person who needs help gets it, regardless of who does the helping. That suggests a truly altruistic motivation. . . .

Batson, incidentally, used to assume that we help others primarily to benefit ourselves. But after a decade of studying empathic response to distress, he's changed his mind. "I feel like the bulk of the evidence points in the direction of the existence of altruism," he says.

Altruism in Children

• If we're naturally selfish, why does helping behavior start so early in life? At the age of 10 to 14 months, a baby will often look upset when someone else falls down or cries. Obviously made unhappy by another person's unhappiness, the child may seek solace in the mother's lap. In the second year, the child will begin comforting in a rudimentary way, such as by patting the head of someone who seems to be in pain. "The frequency (of this behavior) will vary, but most kids will do it sometimes," says Eisenberg.

By the time children are 3 or 4, prosocial behavior is common. One group of researchers videotaped 26 3-to-5-year-olds during 30 hours of free play and recorded about 1,200 acts of sharing, helping, comforting and cooperating. Children can be selfish and mean, too, of course, but there's no reason to think that these characteristics are more common or "natural" than their prosocial inclinations.

Psychologist Hoffman points to two studies showing that newborns cried much more intensely at the sound of another baby's cry than at other, equally loud noises. "That isn't what I'd call empathy," he concedes, "but it is evidence of a primitive precursor to it. There's a basic human tendency to be responsive to other persons' needs, not just your own."

Selfish Genes?

Hoffman rejects biological theories that claim altruism amounts to nothing more than "selfish genes" trying to preserve themselves by prompting the individual to help relatives who share those genes. But he does believe "there may be a biological basis for a disposition to altruism. Natural selection demanded that humans evolve as creatures disposed toward helping, rescuing, protecting others in danger" as well as toward looking out for their own needs.

According to Hoffman, the inborn mechanism that forms the basis for altruism is empathy, which he defines as feeling something more appropriate to someone else's situation than to your own. The way he sees it, empathy becomes increasingly more sophisticated as we grow. First, infants are unable to draw sharp boundaries between themselves and others and sometimes react to another's distress as if they, themselves, had been hurt.

By about 18 months, children can distinguish between "me" and "not-me" but will still assume that others' feelings will be similar to their own. That's why if Jason sees his mother cry out in pain, he may fetch his bottle to make her feel better. By age 2 or 3, it is possible to understand that others react differently and also to empathize with more complex emotions.

Finally, older children can feel for another person's life condition, understanding that his or her distress may be chronic or recognizing that the distress may result from being part of a class of people who are oppressed.

Other psychologists, meanwhile, believe that you are more likely to help others not only if you feel their pain but also if you understand the way the world looks to them. This is called "role-taking" or "perspective-taking." "When people put themselves in the shoes of others, they may become more inclined to render them aid," according to Canadian researchers Dennis Krebs and Cristine Russell.

When they asked an 8-year-old boy named Adam whether that seemed right to him, he replied as follows: "Oh yes, what you do is, you forget everything else that's in your head, and then you make your mind into their mind. Then you know how they're feeling, so you know how to help them."

Some people seem more inclined than others to take Adam's advice—and, in general, to be prosocially oriented. Staub has found that such people have three defining characteristics: They have a positive view of people in general, they are concerned about others' welfare and they take personal responsibility for how other people are doing.

All these, but particularly the first, are affected by the kind of culture one lives in. "It's difficult to lead a competitive, individualistic life"—as we're raised to do in American society—"without devaluing others to some extent," says Staub. So raising children to triumph over others in school and at play is a good way to snuff out their inclination to help.

It appears, then, that caring about others is as much a part of human nature as caring about ourselves. Which impulse gets emphasized is a matter of training, according to the experts. "We fundamentally have the potential to develop into caring, altruistic people or violent, aggressive people," says Staub. "No one will be altruistic if their experiences teach them to be concerned only about themselves. But human connection is intrinsically satisfying if we allow it to be."

> *"First take decent care of yourself, and then you can turn to those who deserve your help."*

Self-Interest Promotes Moral Behavior

Tibor R. Machan

Tibor R. Machan teaches at the Argyros School of Business and Economics at Chapman University in Orange, California. He is also the author of *Human Agency and Society*. In the following viewpoint Machan argues that authentic morality is rooted in self-interest rather than altruism. Only when we have tended to our own needs first can we be of genuine benefit to others, he maintains. Those who act altruistically may mean well, but unless their actions yield good results, their intentions are worthless. But when we help ourselves first, we are generally more successful at helping others, Machan concludes.

As you read, consider the following questions:
1. What analogy does Machan use to illustrate the morality of self-interest?
2. In the author's opinion, why does Mother Teresa's moral system deserve criticism?
3. Why is altruism so widely praised, according to Machan?

Tibor R. Machan, "Self Before Others," *Free Inquiry*, vol. 21, Fall 2001, p. 18.

Now, I am the last guy on Earth to take my clues about life from government regulators. Yet, there are exceptions even to this rule: I ran across one candidate on a recent flight from Orange County to San Jose, California.

If you've ever flown, you probably remember the flight attendants' emergency instructions, delivered before each takeoff: "If we lose air pressure, the oxygen mask will drop from above, and, if you are sitting next to a child, first apply the mask to yourself and then help the kid," or something to that effect. This is one of the few examples in popular culture where it is recognized that, in order to be an effective beneficiary to other people who need one's assistance, one must first be good to oneself—to have rendered oneself fit and able to help. In other words, even the most altruistic sentiments can only bear fruit after certain egoistic needs have been satisfied.

Help Yourself First

No doubt the matter is a bit more complicated. Those who believe that our lives ought first and foremost be devoted to helping the needy believe that what counts most is what we intend to result from our conduct. This is often expressed as the platitude "It's the thought that counts." But, of course, no help that is merely intended achieves very much. What matters is whether the help actually yields results. As it turns out, help toward others that isn't preceded by help toward oneself cannot very often succeed. Inept, unskilled, merely well-meaning folks tend to be of little use to themselves or others.

While many preachers of morality endorse altruism, even they sometimes realize that, unless you love and thus care for yourself first, you cannot love anyone else very effectively. For example, take psychology: the therapies and self-help programs to which millions flock usually make no bones about advocating out-and-out selfishness—of a decent variety, to be sure, not some crass, fictional, brutal selfishness of the sort presented in bad movies like *Erin Brockovich* or *Wall Street*. Instead, most therapies and self-help regimens encourage people to be good to themselves in intelligent, nondestructive ways. No one is met by his or her shrink with the words, "Now let me help you over the next

Humans Are Fundamentally Self-Interested

Notwithstanding any precepts that say we should be other-wise, human beings appear to be intrinsically concerned first with their own welfare.

Hans Selye has argued that the desire to maintain oneself and stay happy is the most ancient—and one of the most important—impulses that motivates living beings. All living beings protect their own interests first of all. Selye points out that this begins with our basic biological make-up, in that the various cells in our bodies only cooperate with each other to ensure their own survival. . . .

It appears that like self-interest, social interest is also inherent within human beings—both have biological roots. Collaboration between body cells promotes the survival of each individual cell and enables the total organism to function.

In effect, individual interests are best served by mutual cooperation. Accordingly, self-interest without social interest is misguided. So is social interest without self-interest. Always putting others first leads to resentment or a martyr attitude. People who believe they are acting purely in the interests of others are dangerous. By denying (to themselves) that their own self-interest is involved, such people may justify all types of manipulative and controlling behavior toward others.

You are both self-interested and socially interested. This dual tendency is built in to your very being and begins with your basic biology. By accepting this about yourself, you will be able to do a better job of acting in your own interests—in an enlightened manner.

Smartrecovery.org, "Enlightened Self," 2004.

several months to get you to practice effective self-sacrifice!" Any such practitioners would lose their lucrative jobs in a jiffy if they did that, and rightly so.

Mother Teresa Versus Bill Gates

But, in the moral system most commonly preached, the story goes otherwise. Mother Teresa was the saint she was, not because she did well for herself—although she did keep saying that she drew great satisfaction from her work, as do most folks who have made it their vocation to help others—but because she meant well for others. It may be, as some have suggested, that Bill Gates is actually doing much more for humanity than Mother Teresa ever did, by creating jobs and tools by which the lives of millions have improved measurably. But because he presumably did this, at least initially, so as to enrich himself, it doesn't count for much in the calculus of popular moral ideals. The fact that Mother Teresa merely helped folks to get by from one day to the next and never tried to set them on some long-term successful course of living doesn't matter, so long as she meant well!

Such a moral system, which actually results in dependence and personal ineptitude unless confined to mere emergency situations, bears serious scrutiny and, yes, criticism. That federally mandated announcement made on every passenger plane gives us a clue as to how a genuine morality must operate: First take decent care of yourself, and then you can turn to those who deserve your help. Practiced conscientiously by everyone, this makes much better sense than the far more popular altruism to which most people give lip service.

Results Matter Most

One thing remains to ponder: if altruism is impractical and confusing, why is it so widely preached? The answer may be that, when moral matters are considered publicly, we tend to focus on what other people can do for us. Nice folks do good service; we thank them when they help us out, whereas if they do well for themselves, we tend not to notice. It matters little to me that you are good to yourself but rather how nice you are to me. So when public debate turns to moral matters, the focus drifts toward generosity, benevolence, charity—the virtues of intention—and away from prudence, courage, and moderation, the virtues that aid one toward self improvement. And so the part of morality that guides us in our relationships to other people tends to get top billing and people mistake the part for the whole.

However, on airplanes—and anywhere else where it is results, not intentions, that matter most—then the wiser course is clear: first genuinely love yourself; then only can you be an effective lover of others!

CHAPTER 5

What Principles Should Guide Our Lives?

Chapter Preface

Perusing the self-help sections in bookstores reveals that people are continually seeking advice on improving their lives. Titles such as Theodore Bryant's *Self-Discipline in 10 Days*, Deepak Chopra's *The Seven Spiritual Laws of Success*, and Martha and William Piepers' *Addicted to Unhappiness* hint at the yearning and dissatisfaction that weaves through modern life. Many people, apparently, seek methods, tenets, and words of wisdom that will guide them toward some higher level of experience, knowledge, or achievement. This chapter considers some of the ideals that notable thinkers have proposed for themselves and others.

The first viewpoint, by Robert Ringer, offers a direct, "no-nonsense" answer to the question of how one should live. Ringer states that it is possible to achieve a "simple, un-complicated life" by "looking out for number one"—that is, rationally pursuing what gives us the most pleasure. To do so, Ringer explains, we must reject certain values and morals that others try to impose on us—particularly the notion that we should sacrifice for others. He is confident that if everyone followed his formula for life, humans would find social harmony as well as personal happiness. In contrast, Ole Hallesby maintains that people should model themselves after Jesus Christ by dedicating their lives to loving and serving others. Hallesby rejects the concept of living solely for one's own happiness, explaining that the life he led before accepting Jesus was "inhuman" and full of "petty selfishness, pride, and pleasure." Since Jesus offers the path to truth, Hallesby contends, truth-seekers ultimately find happiness in living as Jesus lived.

Political philosopher Niccolò Machiavelli does not appear to be interested in seeking truth but in securing power. Like Robert Ringer, his intention is to recommend a simple and practical course of action to achieve success. Unlike Ringer, however, Machiavelli argues that a powerful leader should use *any* means—including hypocrisy, deceit, repression, and cruelty—to maintain supremacy. Machiavelli was writing specifically to the Medici princes of the 1500s to encourage them to save threatened Italian principalities from

French and Spanish military incursions. He may have believed that the Medicis would use their power for the betterment of society. But his argument that "the ends justify the means" suggests that expediency—not morality—is the springboard to success. Thomas Jefferson, on the other hand, contends that honesty and integrity are at the root of happiness and success. In one of his letters, he advises his teenage nephew to "give up money, give up fame, give up science, give [up] the earth itself . . . rather than do an immoral act. And never suppose . . . under any circumstances that it is best for you to do a dishonourable thing." Jefferson's suggestion, perhaps, is that the "means" or actions we take to attain success inevitably shape the "ends" we achieve.

Like Jefferson, Benjamin Franklin focuses on the morality of personal thoughts and actions. In his viewpoint, he discusses his attempt to develop a system to achieve moral perfection in his private life. While admitting his failure, Franklin maintains that his effort was worth it because he learned more about his weaknesses and became a better person. Conversely, Buddhist nun Pema Chödrön advises people to abandon hopes of attaining perfection. In her view, focusing on future potential causes us to ignore our present strengths and weaknesses and creates a life of illusion. Accepting ourselves as we are, she contends, leads to humility and compassion.

Volumes have been written on what principles best guide our choices. While this chapter includes just a few of these precepts, the viewpoints here represent some of the perennial answers to the question of how we should live our lives.

> *"Looking out for Number One is important because it leads to a simple, uncomplicated life in which you spend more time doing those things which give you the greatest amount of pleasure."*

Look Out for Number One

Robert Ringer

In the following viewpoint Robert Ringer maintains that one's goal in life should be to spend time pursuing pleasure as long as this pursuit does not violate the rights of others. Seeking what is in our own best interest; that is, "looking out for number one," is the most rational path to take because it is in accord with the laws of nature, Ringer contends. It benefits the individual because he or she finds happiness; it also benefits others because there are fewer unhappy people to become burdens to society. Ringer, a motivational speaker and author, has written several books, including *Looking Out for Number One* (1977), *Getting What You Want: Seven Principles of Rational Living* (2000), and *Action! Nothing Happens Until Something Moves* (2004).

As you read, consider the following questions:

1. What do "Absolute Moralists" have a tendency to do, according to Ringer?
2. In the author's view, what is the difference between "looking out for Number One" and hedonism?
3. What is wrong with self-sacrifice, in Ringer's opinion?

Robert Ringer, *Looking Out for Number One*. Los Angeles: Los Angeles Book Corporation, 1977. Copyright © 1977 by HarperCollins Publishers. Reproduced by permission.

Before moving forward, it will be extremely helpful to you to attempt to clear your mind of all preconceived ideas, whether they concern friendship, love, business or any other aspect of life. I realize this is easier said than done, but do try to make the effort; it will be worth your while. . . .

Clear your mind, then. Forget foundationless traditions, forget the "moral" standards others may have tried to cram down your throat, forget the beliefs people may have tried to intimidate you into accepting as "right." Allow your intellect to take control as you read, and, most important, think of yourself—Number One—as a unique individual. . . .

Rational Happiness

Looking out for Number One is the conscious, rational effort to spend as much time as possible doing those things which bring you the greatest amount of pleasure and less time on those which cause pain. Everyone automatically makes the effort to be happy, so the key word is "rational.". . .

Because people always do that which they *think* will bring them the greatest pleasure, selfishness is not the issue. Therefore, when people engage in what appear to be altruistic acts, they are not being selfless, as they might like to believe (and might like to have you believe). What they are doing is acting with a lack of awareness. Either they are not completely aware of what they're doing, or they are not aware of why they're doing it, or both. In any case, they are acting selfishly—but not rationally. . . .

Feeling Good

Why is it important to act out of choice? What's in it for you? You already know: more pleasure and less pain—a better life for Number One.

In everyday terms, it means feeling refreshed instead of tired. It means making enough money to be able comfortably to afford the material things you want out of life instead of being bitter about not having them. It means enjoying love relationships instead of longing for them. It means experiencing warm friendships instead of concentrating your thoughts on people for whom you harbor negative feelings. It means feeling healthy instead of lousy. It means having a relatively clear mind instead of one that is cluttered and confused. It means more free time instead of never enough time.

Looking out for Number One is important because it leads to a simple, uncomplicated life in which you spend more time doing those things which give you the greatest amount of pleasure. . . .

When you experience pleasure or an absence of pain, you know one thing: you're *feelin' good.*

When you boil it all down, I think that's what everyone's main objective in life really is—to feel good. Happiness isn't a mysterious condition that needs to be dissected carefully by wordologists or psychologists. It's your state of mind when you're experiencing something pleasurable; it's when you feel good.

We sometimes lose sight of the fact that our primary objective is really to be as happy as possible and that all our other objectives, great and small, are only a means to that end. . . .

The Absolute Moralist

Is looking out for Number One "right?" As a preface, I find it necessary to describe an old nemesis of mine—a creature who's been running around loose on Planet Earth over the millennia, steadily increasing in number. He is the Absolute Moralist. His mission in life is to whip you and me into line. Like Satan, he disguises himself in various human forms. He may appear as a politician on one occasion, next as a minister, and still later as your mother-in-law.

Whatever his disguise, he is relentless. He'll stalk you to your grave if you let him. If he senses that you're one of his prey—that you do not base your actions on rational self-choice—he'll punish you unmercifully. He will make guilt your bedfellow until you're convinced you're a bad guy.

The Absolute Moralist is the creature—looking deceptively like any ordinary human being—who spends his life deciding what is right for *you.* If he gives to charity, he'll try to shame you into "understanding" that it's your moral duty to give to charity too (usually the charity of his choice). If he believes in Christ, he's certain that it's his moral duty to help you "see the light." (In the most extreme cases, he may even feel morally obliged to kill you in order to "save" you from your disbelief.) If he doesn't smoke or drink, it takes little effort for him "logically" to conclude that smoking and drinking are wrong for you. In essence, all he wants is to run your life. There is only one thing which can frustrate him into leaving you alone, and that is your firm decision never to allow him to impose his beliefs on you.

Eliminate the Moral Opinions of Others

In deciding whether it's right to look out for Number One, I suggest that the first thing you do is eliminate from consideration all unsolicited moral opinions of others. Morality—the quality of character—is a very personal and private matter. No other living person has the right to decide what is moral (right or wrong) for you. I further suggest that you make a prompt and thorough effort to eliminate from your life all individuals who claim—by words or actions, directly or by inference—to possess such a right. You should concern yourself only with whether looking out for Number One is moral from your own rational, aware viewpoint.

Rational Self-Interest

In popular usage, the word "selfishness" is a synonym of evil; the image it conjures is of a murderous brute who tramples over piles of corpses to achieve his own ends, who cares for no living being and pursues nothing but the gratification of the mindless whims of any immediate moment.

Yet the exact meaning and dictionary definition of the word "selfishness" is: *concern with one's own interests*. . . .

Just as man cannot survive by any random means, but must discover and practice the principles which his survival requires, so man's self-interest cannot be determined by blind desires or random whims, but must be discovered and achieved by the guidance of rational principles. . . .

Since selfishness is "concern with one's own interests,". . . [the] attack on "selfishness" is an attack on man's self-esteem; to surrender one, is to surrender the other.

Ayn Rand, *The Virtue of Selfishness*, 1961.

Looking out for Number One means spending more time doing those things which give you pleasure. It does not, however, give you carte blanche to do whatever you please. It is not hedonistic in concept, because the looking-out-for-Number-One philosophy does not end with the hedonistic assertion that man's primary moral duty lies in the pursuit of pleasure.

Looking out for Number One adds a rational, civilized tag: man's primary moral duty lies in the pursuit of pleasure *so long as he does not forcibly interfere with the rights of others.* . . .

There is a rational reason why forcible interference with others has no place in the philosophy of looking out for Number One. It's simply not in your best interest. In the long run it will bring you more pain than pleasure—the exact opposite of what you wish to accomplish. It's possible that you may, on occasion, experience short-term pleasure by violating the rights of others, but I assure you that the long-term losses (i.e., pain) from such actions will more than offset any short-term enjoyment. . . .

With absolute morality and hedonism out of the way, I perhaps can best answer the question *Is it right?* by asking you one: Can you see any rational reason why you *shouldn't* try to make your life more pleasurable and less painful, so long as you do not forcibly interfere with the rights of others?

You have but one life to live. Is there anything unreasonable about watching over that life carefully and doing everything within your power to make it a pleasant and fulfilling one? Is it wrong to be aware of what you're doing and why you're doing it? Is it evil to act out of free choice rather than out of the choice of others or out of blind chance?

Avoid Self-Sacrifice

Remember, selfishness is not the issue. So-called self-sacrifice is just an irrationally selfish act (doing what you think will make you feel good) committed under the influence of a low awareness level. The truth is that it won't make you feel good—certainly not in the long run, after bitterness over what you've "sacrificed" has had a chance to fester within you. At its extreme, this bitterness eventually can develop into a serious case of absolute moralitis. A person's irrational decision to be self-sacrificial can lead to a bitterness so great that it can be soothed only by his preaching to others the virtue of committing the same error.

You may mean well, but don't try so hard to sacrifice for others. It's unfair to them and a disaster for you. The sad irony is that if you persist in swimming in the dangerous and uncivilized waters of self-sacrifice, those for whom you "sacrifice" often will be worse off for your efforts. If instead you spend your time looking out for Number One, those people for whom you care most will benefit by your actions. It's only when you try to pervert the laws of Nature and make the other person's happiness your first responsibility, relegating yourself to the Number Two position, that you run into trouble. It has never worked, and it will not work for you. It's a law of Nature. The idea that self-sacrifice is virtuous is a law of man. If you're going to expend your energies fighting laws, fight man-made laws; they are worth resisting. The laws of Nature will not budge an inch no matter how great your efforts.

That looking out for Number One brings happiness to others, in addition to Number One, is one of the beautiful realities of life. At best, it benefits you and one or more other persons. At worst, it benefits only you and interferes with no one else. Even in the latter case, it actually is a benefit to others because the happy individual is one more person on this earth who does not represent a potential burden to the rest of the population.

That, in my opinion, is enough to make it right. If you practice the principles of looking out for Number One, you'll find it easier to develop rewarding relationships with other human beings, both friends and lovers. It will enhance your ability to be a warm and sensitive person and to enjoy all that life has to offer.

> *"He sought the welfare of others to such an extent that He was oblivious of Himself if only He might do some good to others."*

Live for Others as Jesus Did

Ole Hallesby

Ole Hallesby (1879–1961) was a prominent Christian theologian, teacher, and writer in Norway. In the following viewpoint, excerpted from his book *Why I Am a Christian*, Hallesby explains that humans have continually sought to find the meaning of life in various religious systems. He contends that each system proved to be unsatisfactory in some way—until the appearance of Jesus Christ. Hallesby maintains that Jesus is unique in the history of religion because his life was the ultimate expression of how humans were meant to live. Jesus's legacy—a life lived in service to others—is the most satisfying model for humans, Hallesby concludes.

As you read, consider the following questions:

1. How does Hallesby define the word *conscience*?
2. In the author's opinion, how did Jesus differ from the religious leaders who preceded him?
3. What does Hallesby say his life was like before he came to learn about Jesus?

Ole Hallesby, *Why I Am a Christian*, translated by Clarence J. Carlsen. Minneapolis, MN: Augsburg Publishing House, 1930. Copyright © 1930, renewed in 1958 by Clarence J. Carlsen. Reproduced by permission.

Human life has its own peculiar characteristics, which make it human. And this life develops only under certain conditions and in certain environments.

One of the characteristics of human life, among others, is that it must discover its own peculiarity; that is, discover the meaning of life. In all other living beings the innate life unfolds itself automatically, by means of the instincts. In man, however, the unfolding of life takes place consciously and deliberately.

Man himself must know what it means to be a man, and will to be it. He himself must select the environment in which his own peculiar life can unfold itself. And this is what men have been working at down through the ages as far back as we have any historical records of human life. The best men and women of each generation have been the ones who have sacrificed the most time and energy to ascertain the meaning of life.

The Founding of Religions

One day a quiet, good man came forth and said: "I have found it."

Men crowded around him and listened. After they had heard him to the end, they said: "Verily, we have found it!"

And a religion had been founded upon earth.

Now, all life is supplied with a peculiar apparatus which we call sensitiveness or feeling. It constitutes a very important factor in life. It serves life both positively and negatively. It serves positively by making the living organism aware of those things or conditions which will promote its existence. Even in plants we can clearly discern a "sensitiveness" of this kind. If a tree, for instance, is growing in lean earth and there is better earth a short distance away, we notice that the tree practically moves away from the lean earth by sending its roots over into the good earth.

The feelings serve the living organism negatively by making it aware of everything in its surroundings which is detrimental to its existence. Thus, for instance, the sensitiveness of our skin. It helps us to protect our bodies against dangerous cold or heat. If we touch a hot iron, our feelings give instant warning and we withdraw our hand, thereby escaping greater injury. . . .

The Conscience

Our soul-life, too, has its apparatus for feeling, the function of which is to serve this life by pointing out those things in our environment which are conducive to the well being of the soul and by warning against those things which are detrimental to it. This apparatus of the soul we usually call the conscience. It is a part of that life which is peculiar to man, and a very important part, because it is the life-preserving and life-protecting function of the soul.

Its task is to prove all things both from without and within which affect our spiritual life and to determine whether they are beneficial or detrimental to the soul. If the conscience is permitted to function normally, nothing reaches the soul before the conscience has expressed its opinion concerning it.

When the quiet, good man had spoken, and men had heard from him what the meaning of life was, conscience immediately began its work. It proved all things. But gradually the number of those grew greater and greater who said to themselves and later to others: this is not the meaning of life.

And they began anew to try to find the answer to the old problem.

One day another man came forth. He, too, was a quiet and a good man. He, too, said: "I have found it."

And people listened and said: "In truth, now we have found it."

And another new religion had been founded on earth.

Thus it continued through hundreds and thousands of years. But the conscience of man was not satisfied with any of the solutions.

The True Meaning of Life

Then came Jesus.

He showed us what the meaning of life is. When Jesus came, we saw for the first time on earth what a real man is. He called himself the *"Son of Man."*

The others, who had preceded Jesus, could only tell us how a man should be. Jesus, however, exemplified it in His own life. He did not only point out the ideal, as others had done; He Himself was the ideal, and He actually lived it out before our very eyes.

Permit me to mention two things in connection with this ideal. In the first place, Jesus, too, directs His appeal to our consciences. Furthermore, He seeks no other following but that which the consciences of men will grant Him.

Many think that Jesus forces men to follow Him. In so doing they reveal how little they know about Him.

Living for Others

Open the Gospel to almost any page, and you will find Jesus dealing with someone. It might be an individual, it might be a crowd, but in the scene Jesus is doing something for someone. He is forgiving sins, healing diseases, freeing people from their fears, feeding a crowd, calming a storm, teaching or answering questions, inviting or encouraging someone. He might also be confronting religious and political leaders, but even this will be in the interest of oppressed people. The Lutheran theologian Dietrich Bonhoeffer calls Jesus "the man for others." He is devoted to relieving human misery. He spends himself in service. What is amazing in Jesus is the universality of his love, his reverence for all persons no matter who they are, his ability to see the good, his desire that all people enjoy inner and outer freedom and fullness of life. . . .

Jesus lays great stress on our relationships with one another, and here too what he teaches is what he lives. Our love should extend to all, even to those who hate us, malign us, oppress us or persecute us. We should pray for them, and do good to them (Mt 5). . . . Jesus teaches us to love the poor, even to the extent of selling all we have and giving it to them (Mk 10). . . . We should feed the hungry, give drink to the thirsty, welcome the stranger, clothe the naked, visit those who are ill or in prison (Mt 25). We should serve one another.

Thomas N. Hart, *To Know and Follow Jesus*, 1984.

Let me call your attention to one incident in the life of Jesus. It was during the great awakening in Galilee. The people were streaming together and almost trampling one another down. One day Jesus stopped and looked at all these people. And He seemed to ask Himself this question: I wonder if they have understood me? Then He turned and cried out once again to the multitudes: "No man can be my disciple without renouncing all that he hath, yea, even his own life" (Luke 14:25–33).

A man who speaks to the people in that way does not expect to gain any other adherents but such as are convinced in their hearts that both the man and his message are trustworthy and that they, therefore, are inwardly bound to follow him, regardless of what it may cost them.

This is the remarkable thing that happens. When our consciences are confronted by Jesus, we are compelled to accord Him our full and unqualified approval. At least, He received the approval of my conscience. No matter in what situation I see Jesus, my conscience says: Verily, that is the way a man should be. . . .

The Life of Jesus

What, then, was the life of Jesus like?

Large volumes, both scientific and devotional, have, of course, been written about this. I must be brief and shall, therefore, mention only a couple of the fundamental traits, the two which, to my mind, most clearly distinguish the life of Jesus from that of all other people.

In the first place, Jesus never had to grope His way to find the meaning of life, as everybody else has had to do, both before and after His time. Unerringly He discerned it and lived in harmony with it, to Him a perfectly natural way of living. We cannot discover that He was ever in doubt, not even during His temptation or His passion.

The unique thing about Jesus, however, that which impresses us most, was, without comparison, His intimate and unbroken fellowship with the Father. He Himself knew that this was the secret of his life. . . .

In the second place, I would mention the life Jesus lived among men.

The unique thing about this aspect of His life, as contrasted with our lives, was that He sought the welfare of others to such an extent that He was oblivious of Himself if only He might do some good to others.

Jesus has had many enemies, both among His contemporaries and since, and they have scrutinized His life very closely. None of them, however, has been able to point to a single instance in which Jesus acted from selfish motives.

Jesus has given expression to this normal human life by

saying: "Thou shalt love the Lord thy God above all else, and thy neighbor as thyself.". . .

The Choice

Permit me at this point to mention the two things which came to mean most to me.

In the first place, concerning the life of Jesus with which I had now come in contact, my conscience compelled me to say: Verily, that is the way a man should be. I began to feel also that the life of Jesus was a condemnation of my own life. . . .

I now saw how inhuman the life was which I had been living. Jesus lived His life for others. I had lived my whole life for myself, in petty selfishness, pride, and pleasure. . . .

In the second place, the life of Jesus attracted me with a power which I had never before felt in all my life.

I saw before my eyes that pure, good, beautiful, and strong life which God had intended that I should live. It attracted me with a wonderful power.

I could understand now why so many young men were drawn to Jesus. All He had to say to them was: "Follow me," and they left all and followed Him. . . .

Jesus once said: "Everyone that is of the truth heareth my voice." Now I knew that Jesus was right. Every one who is confronted by Jesus and refuses to accept Him is untrue to himself.

I had formerly believed that people who became Christians had to deny their own convictions, if they were people who did their own thinking, but now I saw that I had to become a Christian if I was not to be untrue to myself and my most sacred convictions.

Then came the choice.

I had to choose. . . .

I could not endure being untrue to myself, both for time and for eternity. I could not enter upon a life of unequivocal falsehood, such as would have been the case if, after having been confronted with Jesus, I had continued to live as before.

So I chose to follow Jesus.

> *"It is well to seem merciful, faithful, humane, sincere, religious, and also to be so; but you must have the mind so disposed that when it is needful . . . you may be able to change to the opposite qualities."*

Develop a Devious Mind

Niccolò Machiavelli

A native of Florence, Italy, Niccolò Machiavelli (1469–1527) was a diplomat, government administrator, and political theorist during the rule of the rich and culturally influential Medici family. His famous book *The Prince*, from which the following viewpoint is excerpted, was written as practical advice to the Medici princes to aid them in governing. Machiavelli argues that a successful ruler must learn to manipulate others, using any means, including deceit, to gain and maintain power. A powerful leader should seem good and honorable if it serves his purposes; he should also appear cruel and be willing to commit evil acts when the need arises.

As you read, consider the following questions:

1. In Machiavelli's opinion, is it safer to be feared or loved?
2. Why must a ruler learn to imitate both the fox and the lion, according to the author?
3. What is the most necessary quality that a leader should appear to have, in Machiavelli's view?

Niccolò Machiavelli, *The Prince*, translated by Luigi Ricci. New York: Random House, 1950.

It now remains to be seen what are the methods and rules for a prince as regards his subjects and friends. And as I know that many have written of this, I fear that my writing about it may be deemed presumptuous, differing as I do, especially in this matter, from the opinions of others. But my intention being to write something of use to those who understand, it appears to me more proper to go to the real truth of the matter than to its imagination; and many have imagined republics and principalities which have never been seen or known to exist in reality; for how we live is so far removed from how we ought to live, that he who abandons what is done for what ought to be done, will rather learn to bring about his own ruin than his preservation. A man who wishes to make a profession of goodness in everything must necessarily come to grief among so many who are not good. Therefore it is necessary for a prince, who wishes to maintain himself, to learn how not to be good, and to use this knowledge and not use it, according to the necessity of the case. . . .

Love or Fear as Motives

From this arises the question whether it is better to be loved more than feared, or feared more than loved. The reply is, that one ought to be both feared and loved, but as it is difficult for the two to go together, it is much safer to be feared than loved, if one of the two has to be wanting. For it may be said of men in general that they are ungrateful, voluble, dissemblers, anxious to avoid danger, and covetous of gain; as long as you benefit them, they are entirely yours; they offer you their blood, their goods, their life, and their children, as I have before said, when the necessity is remote; but when it approaches, they revolt. And the prince who has relied solely on their words, without making other preparations, is ruined; for the friendship which is gained by purchase and not through grandeur and nobility of spirit is bought but not secured, and at a pinch is not to be expended in your service. And men have less scruple in offending one who makes himself loved than one who makes himself feared; for love is held by a chain of obligation which, men being selfish, is broken whenever it serves their purpose; but fear is maintained by a dread of punishment which never fails.

Still, a prince should make himself feared in such a way that if he does not gain love, he at any rate avoids hatred; for fear and the absence of hatred may well go together, and will be always attained by one who abstains from interfering with the property of his citizens and subjects or with their women. And when he is obliged to take the life of any one, let him do so when there is a proper justification and manifest reason for it; but above all he must abstain from taking the property of others, for men forget more easily the death of their father than the loss of their patrimony [inheritance]. . . .

But when the prince is with his army and has a large number of soldiers under his control, then it is extremely necessary that he should not mind being thought cruel; for without this reputation he could not keep an army united or disposed to any duty. Among the noteworthy actions of Hannibal is numbered this, that although he had an enormous army, composed of men of all nations and fighting in foreign countries, there never arose any dissension either among them or against the prince, either in good fortune or in bad. This could not be due to anything but his inhuman cruelty, which together with his infinite other virtues, made him always venerated and terrible in the sight of his soldiers, and without it his other virtues would not have sufficed to produce that effect. Thoughtless writers admire on the one hand his actions, and on the other blame the principal cause of them. . . .

I conclude, therefore, with regard to being feared and loved, that men love at their own free will, but fear at the will of the prince, and that a wise prince must rely on what is in his power and not on what is in the power of others, and he must only contrive to avoid incurring hatred, as has been explained.

Honesty and Trickery

How laudable it is for a prince to keep good faith and live with integrity, and not with astuteness, every one knows. Still, the experience of our times shows those princes to have done great things who have had little regard for good faith, and have been able by astuteness to confuse men's brains, and who have ultimately overcome those who have made loyalty their foundation. . . .

A prince being thus obliged to know well how to act as a

beast must imitate the fox and the lion, for the lion cannot protect himself from traps, and the fox cannot defend himself from wolves. One must therefore be a fox to recognise traps, and a lion to frighten wolves. Those that wish to be only lions do not understand this. Therefore, a prudent ruler ought not to keep faith when by so doing it would be against his interest, and when the reasons which made him bind himself no longer exist. If men were all good, this precept would not be a good one; but as they are bad, and would not observe their faith with you, so you are not bound to keep faith with them. Nor have legitimate grounds ever failed a prince who wished to show colourable excuse for the non-fulfilment of his promise. Of this one could furnish an infinite number of modern examples, and show how many times peace has been broken, and how many promises rendered worthless, by the faithlessness of princes, and those that have been best able to imitate the fox have succeeded best. But it is necessary to be able to disguise this character well, and to be a great feigner and dissembler; and men are so simple and so ready to obey present necessities, that one who deceives will always find those who allow themselves to be deceived.

Browne. © by King Features Syndicate, Inc. Reproduced by permission.

I will only mention one modern instance. [Pope] Alexander VI did nothing else but deceive men, he thought of nothing else, and found the occasion for it; no man was ever more able to give assurances, or affirmed things with stronger oaths, and no man observed them less; however, he always succeeded in his deceptions, as he well knew this aspect of things.

It is not, therefore, necessary for a prince to have all the above-named qualities, but it is very necessary to seem to have them. I would even be bold to say that to possess them and always to observe them is dangerous, but to appear to possess them is useful. Thus it is well to seem merciful, faithful, humane, sincere, religious, and also to be so; but you must have the mind so disposed that when it is needful to be otherwise you may be able to change to the opposite qualities. And it must be understood that a prince, and especially a new prince, cannot observe all those things which are considered good in men, being often obliged, in order to maintain the state, to act against faith, against charity, against humanity, and against religion. And, therefore, he must have a mind disposed to adapt itself according to the wind, and as the variations of fortune dictate, and, as I said before, not deviate from what is good, if possible, but be able to do evil if constrained.

A prince must take great care that nothing goes out of his mouth which is not full of the above-named five qualities, and, to see and hear him, he should seem to be all mercy, faith, integrity, humanity, and religion. And nothing is more necessary than to seem to have this last quality, for men in general judge more by the eyes than by the hands, for every one can see, but very few have to feel. Everybody sees what you appear to be, few feel what you are, and those few will not dare to oppose themselves to the many, who have the majesty of the state to defend them; and in the actions of men, and especially of princes, from which there is no appeal, the end justifies the means. Let a prince therefore aim at conquering and maintaining the state, and the means will always be judged honourable and praised by every one, for the vulgar is always taken by appearances and the issue of the event; and the world consists only of the vulgar, and the few who are not vulgar are isolated when the many have a rallying point in the prince. A certain prince of the present time, whom it is well not to name, never does anything but preach peace and good faith, but he is really a great enemy to both, and either of them, had he observed them, would have lost him state or reputation on many occasions.

"Pursue the interests of your country, the interests of your friends, and your own interests also with the purest integrity, the most chaste honour."

Develop an Honest Heart

Thomas Jefferson

The primary author of the Declaration of Independence, Thomas Jefferson (1743–1826), served as secretary of state under George Washington before becoming the second vice president and the third president of the United States. The following viewpoint is taken from a 1785 letter to Peter Carr, Jefferson's fifteen-year-old nephew and ward. In this letter Jefferson urges Carr to pursue honesty and virtue above all other goals. He maintains that even private actions should be rooted in integrity and that habitual lying is the most despicable offense. Following honesty, intellectual growth, moral development, and physical health are also of significant value, writes Jefferson.

As you read, consider the following questions:
1. What does Jefferson say one must give up before committing an immoral act?
2. In Jefferson's opinion, what does the "falsehood of the tongue" lead to?
3. What should be the purpose of walking, according to Jefferson?

Thomas Jefferson, letter to his nephew and ward, Peter Carr, August 19, 1785.

Time now begins to be precious to you. Every day you lose, will retard [by] a day your entrance on that public stage whereon you may begin to be useful to yourself. However the way to repair the loss is to improve the future time. I trust that with your dispositions even the acquisition of science is a pleasing employment. I can assure you that the possession of it is what (next to an honest heart) will above all things render you dear to your friends, and give you fame and promotion in your own country. When your mind shall be well improved with science, nothing will be necessary to place you in the highest points of view but to pursue the interests of your country, the interests of your friends, and your own interests also with the purest integrity, the most chaste honour. The defect of these virtues can never be made up by all the other acquirements of body and mind. Make these then your first object.

Exercise Virtue

Give up money, give up fame, give up science, give [up] the earth itself and all it contains rather than do an immoral act. And never suppose that in any possible situation or under any circumstances that it is best for you to do a dishonourable thing however slightly so it may appear to you. Whenever you are to do a thing tho' it can never be known but to yourself, ask yourself how you would act were all the world looking at you, and act accordingly. Encourage all your virtuous dispositions, and exercise them whenever an opportunity arises, being assured that they will gain strength by exercise as a limb of the body does, and that exercise will make them habitual. From the practice of the purest virtue you may be assured you will derive the most sublime comforts in every moment of life and in the moment of death. If ever you find yourself environed with difficulties and perplexing circumstances, out of which you are at a loss how to extricate yourself, do what is right, and be assured that that will extricate you the best out of the worst situations. Tho' you cannot see when you fetch one step, what will be the next, yet follow truth, justice, and plain-dealing, and never fear their leading you out of the labyrinth in the easiest manner possible. The knot which you thought a Gordian one will untie itself before you. Nothing is so mistaken as the supposition that a person is to extricate himself from a difficulty, by intrigue, by chicanery, by dissimulation, by trimming, by an untruth, by an injustice. This increases the difficulties tenfold, and those who pursue these methods, get themselves so involved at length that they can turn no way but their infamy becomes more exposed. It is of great importance to set a resolution, not to be shaken, never to tell an untruth. There is no vice so mean, so pitiful, so contemptible and he who permits himself to tell a lie once, finds it much easier to do it a second and third time, till at length it becomes habitual, he tells lies without attending to it, and truths without the world's believing him. This falsehood of the tongue leads to that of the heart, and in time depraves all its good dispositions.

The Second Blessing

An honest heart being the first blessing, a knowing head is the second. It is time for you now to begin to be choice in your reading, to begin to pursue a regular course in it and not to suffer yourself to be turned to the right or left by reading anything out of that course. I have long ago digested a plan for you, suited to the circumstances in which you will be placed. This I will detail to you from time to time as you advance. For the present I advise you to begin a course of ancient history, reading every thing in the original and not in translations. First read Goldsmith's history of Greece. This will give you a digested view of that field. Then take up ancient history in the detail, reading the following books in the following order. Herodotus. Thucydides. Xenophontis *Hellenica*. Xenophontis *Anabasis*. Quintus Curtius. Justin. This shall form the first stage of your historical reading, and is all I need mention to you now. The next will be of Roman history. From that we will come down to Modern history. In Greek and Latin poetry, you have read or will read at school Virgil, Terence, Horace, Anacreon, Theocritus, Homer. Read also Milton's *Paradise Lost*, Ossian, Pope's works, Swift's works in order to form your style in your own language. In morality read Epictetus, Xenophontis' memorabilia, Plato's Socratic dialogues, Cicero's philosophies.

A Strong Body and a Strong Mind

In order to assure a certain progress in this reading, consider what hours you have free from the school and the exercises of the school. Give about two of them every day to exercise; for health must not be sacrificed to learning. A strong body makes the mind strong. . . .

Never think of taking a book with you. The object of walking is to relax the mind. You should therefore not permit yourself even to think while you walk. But divert your attention by the objects surrounding you. Walking is the best possible exercise. Habituate yourself to walk very far. . . .

There is no habit you will value so much as that of walking far without fatigue. I would advise you to take your exercise in the afternoon. Not because it is the best time for exercise for certainly it is not: but because it is the best time to spare from your studies; and habit will soon reconcile it to health, and render it nearly as useful as if you gave to that the more precious hours of the day. A little walk of half an hour in the morning when you first rise is advisable also. It shakes off sleep, and produces other good effects in the animal oeconomy. Rise at a fixed and an early hour, and go to bed at a fixed and early hour also. Sitting up late at night is injurious to the health, and not useful to the mind.

"I conceived the bold and arduous project of arriving at moral perfection. I wished to live without committing any fault at any time."

Aim for Personal Perfection

Benjamin Franklin

Benjamin Franklin (1706–1790) was a jack-of-all-trades: journalist, scientist, inventor, diplomat, statesman, anti-slavery activist—and a member of the committee that helped to draft the U.S. Declaration of Independence. In his autobiography, from which the following viewpoint is taken, Franklin presents his formula for attaining moral perfection. He defines thirteen necessary virtues and designs a daily log to help him keep track of his faults. Franklin also concentrates on mastering one virtue per week. Franklin admits that he never achieved perfection but that his efforts to do so made him a better person.

As you read, consider the following questions:
1. In Franklin's opinion, why should temperance be first on the list of virtues to master?
2. What virtue proved to be the most difficult for Franklin to attain?
3. What virtue did Franklin overlook but later add to his list, at the suggestion of a Quaker friend?

Benjamin Franklin, *The Autobiography of Benjamin Franklin*. Boston: Houghton Mifflin, 1903.

It was about this time I conceived the bold and arduous project of arriving at moral perfection. I wished to live without committing any fault at any time; I would conquer all that either natural inclination, custom, or company might lead me into. As I knew, or thought I knew, what was right and wrong, I did not see why I might not always do the one and avoid the other. But I soon found I had undertaken a task of more difficulty than I had imagined. While my care was employed in guarding against one fault, I was often surprised by another; habit took the advantage of inattention; inclination was sometimes too strong for reason. I concluded, at length, that the mere speculative conviction that it was our interest to be completely virtuous was not sufficient to prevent our slipping; and that the contrary habits must be broken and good ones acquired and established before we can have any dependence on a steady, uniform rectitude of conduct. For this purpose I therefore contrived the following method. . . .

Virtues to Acquire

I concluded under thirteen names of virtues all that at that time occurred to me as necessary or desirable and annexed to each a short precept which fully expressed the extent I gave to its meaning.

These names of virtues with their precepts were:

1. TEMPERANCE

Eat not to dullness; drink not to elevation.

2. SILENCE

Speak not but what may benefit others or yourself; avoid trifling conversation.

3. ORDER

Let all your things have their places; let each part of your business have its time.

4. RESOLUTION

Resolve to perform what you ought; perform without fail what you resolve.

5. FRUGALITY

Make no expense but to do good to others or yourself; i.e., waste nothing.

6. INDUSTRY

Lose no time; be always employed in something useful; cut off all unnecessary actions.

7. SINCERITY

Use no harmful deceit; think innocently and justly, and, if you speak, speak accordingly.

8. JUSTICE

Wrong none by doing injuries or omitting the benefits that are your duty.

9. MODERATION

Avoid extremes; forbear resenting injuries so much as you think they deserve.

10. CLEANLINESS

Tolerate no uncleanliness in body, clothes or habitation.

11. TRANQUILLITY

Be not disturbed at trifles, or at accidents common or unavoidable.

12. CHASTITY

Rarely use venery but for health or offspring, never to dullness, weakness, or the injury of your own or another's peace or reputation.

13. HUMILITY

Imitate Jesus and Socrates.

My intention being to acquire the *habitude* of all these virtues, I judged it would be well not to distract my attention by attempting the whole at once, but to fix it on one of them at a time; and, when I should be master of that, then to proceed to another, and so on, till I should have gone through the thirteen; and, as the previous acquisition of some might facilitate the acquisition of certain others, I arranged them with that view as they stand above. Temperance first, as it tends to procure that coolness and clearness of head which is so necessary where constant vigilance was to be kept up and guard maintained against the unremitting attraction of ancient habits and the force of perpetual temptations. This being acquired and established, Silence would be more easy; and my desire being to gain knowledge at the same time that I improved in virtue, and considering that in conversation it was obtained rather by the use of the ears than of the tongue, and therefore wishing to break a habit I was getting into of prattling, punning, and joking which only made me acceptable to trifling company, I gave Silence the second place. This and the next, Order, I expected would allow me more time for attending to my project and my studies. Resolution, once become habitual, would keep me firm in my endeavors to obtain all the subsequent virtues; Frugality and Industry freeing me from my remaining debt, and producing affluence and independence, would make more easy the practice of Sincerity and Justice, etc., etc. Conceiving then that agreeably to the advice of Pythagoras in his Golden Verses daily examination would be necessary, I contrived the following method for conducting that examination.

I made a little book in which I allotted a page for each of the virtues. I ruled each page with red ink so as to have seven columns, one for each day of the week, marking each column with a letter for the day. I crossed these columns with thirteen red lines, marking the beginning of each line with the first letter of one of the virtues, on which line and in its proper column I might mark by a little black spot, every fault I found upon examination to have been committed respecting that virtue upon that day.

I determined to give a week's strict attention to each of the virtues successively. Thus in the first week my great guard was to avoid even the least offense against Temperance, leaving the other virtues to their ordinary chance, only marking every evening the faults of the day. Thus, if in the first week I could keep my first line, marked T, clear of spots, I supposed the habit of that virtue so much strengthened and its opposite weakened that I might venture extending my attention to include the next, and for the following week keep both lines clear of spots. Proceeding thus to the last, I could go through a course complete in thirteen weeks and four courses in a year. . . .

Ordering My Day

The precept of Order requiring that *every part of my business should have its allotted time,* one page in my little book contained the following scheme of employment for the twenty-four hours of a natural day.

The Morning.			
	5	}	Rise, wash, and address *Powerful Goodness!* Contrive day's business and take the resolution of the day; prosecute the present study, and breakfast.
Question. What good shall I do this day?	6		
	7		
	8	}	Work.
	9		
	10		
	11		
Noon.	12	}	Read, or overlook my accounts, and dine.
	1		
	2	}	Work.
	3		
	4		
	5		
Evening.	6	}	Put things in their places. Supper. Music or diversion, or conversation. Examination of the day.
Question. What good have I done to-day?	7		
	8		
	9		
Night.	10	}	Sleep
	11		
	12		
	1		
	2		
	3		
	4		

I entered upon the execution of this plan for self-examination and continued it with occasional intermissions for some time. I was surprised to find myself so much fuller of faults than I had imagined; but I had the satisfaction of seeing them diminish. To avoid the trouble of renewing now and then my little book, which, by scraping out the marks on the paper of old faults to make room for new ones in a new course, became full of holes, I transferred my tables and precepts to the ivory leaves of a memorandum book on which the lines were drawn with red ink that made a durable stain, and on those lines I marked my faults with a black-lead pencil, which marks I could easily wipe out with a wet sponge. After a while I went through one course only in a year, and afterward only one in several years, till at length I omitted them entirely, being employed in voyages and business abroad with a multiplicity of affairs that interfered; but I always carried my little book with me.

A Speckled Axe Was Best

My scheme of Order gave me the most trouble. . . . I was almost ready to give up the attempt and content myself with a faulty character in that respect, like the man who, in buying an axe of a smith, my neighbor, desired to have the whole of its surface as bright as the edge. The smith consented to grind it bright for him if he would turn the wheel; he turned while the smith pressed the broad face of the axe hard and heavily on the stone, which made the turning of it very fatiguing. The man came every now and then from the wheel to see how the work went on, and at length would take his axe as it was, without farther grinding. "No," said the smith, "turn on, turn on: we shall have it bright by-and-by; as yet, it is only speckled." "Yes," says the man, *but I think I like a speckled axe best."* . . .

In truth, I found myself incorrigible with respect to Order; and now I am grown old and my memory bad, I feel very sensibly the want of it. But on the whole, though I never arrived at the perfection I had been so ambitious of obtaining, but fell far short of it, yet I was by the endeavor a better and a happier man than I otherwise should have been if I had not attempted it.

I Added Humility to My List

My list of virtues contained at first but twelve; but a Quaker friend having kindly informed me that I was generally thought proud; that my pride showed itself frequently in conversation; that I was not content with being in the right when discussing any point, but was overbearing, and rather insolent, of which he convinced me by mentioning several instances; I determined endeavoring to cure myself, if I could, of this vice or folly among the rest, and I added Humility to my list, giving an extensive meaning to the word.

Franklin's Log and Virtues

	S.	M.	T.	W.	T.	F.	S.
TEMPERANCE. EAT NOT TO DULLNESS; DRINK NOT TO ELEVATION.							
T.							
S.	*	*		*		*	
O.	**	*	*		*	*	*
R.		*				*	
F.		*			*		
I.		*					
S.							
J.							
M.							
C.							
T.							
C.							
H.							

These names of virtues with their precepts were:

TEMPERANCE
Eat not to dullness. Drink not to elevation.

SILENCE
Speak not but what may benefit others or yourself. Avoid trifling conversation.

ORDER
Let all your things have their places. Let each part of your business have its time.

RESOLUTION
Resolve to perform what you ought. Perform without fail what you resolve.

FRUGALITY
Make no expense but to do good to others or yourself; i.e., waste nothing.

INDUSTRY
Lose no time. Be always employed in something useful. Cut off all unnecessary actions.

SINCERITY
Use no hurtful deceit. Think innocently and justly; and, if you speak, speak accordingly.

JUSTICE
Wrong none by doing injuries or omitting the benefits that are your duty.

MODERATION
Avoid extremes. Forbear resenting injuries so much as you think they deserve.

CLEANLINESS
Tolerate no uncleanliness in body, clothes or habitation.

TRANQUILLITY
Be not disturbed at trifles or at accidents common or unavoidable.

CHASTITY
Rarely use venery but for health or offspring—never to dullness, weakness, or the injury of your own or another's peace or reputation.

HUMILITY
Imitate Jesus and Socrates.

I cannot boast of much success in acquiring the *reality* of this virtue, but I had a good deal with regard to the *appearance* of it. I made it a rule to forbear all direct contradiction to the sentiments of others and all positive assertion of my own. I even forbade myself, agreeably to the old laws of our Junto, the use of every word or expression in the language that imported a fixed opinion, such as "certainly," "undoubtedly," etc., and I adopted, instead of them, "I conceive," "I apprehend," or "I imagine" a thing to be so or so; or it "so appears to me at present." When another asserted something that I thought an error, I denied myself the pleasure of contradicting him abruptly and of showing immediately some absurdity in his proposition; and in answering I began by observing that in certain cases or circumstances his opinion would be right, but in the present case there *appeared* or *seemed* to me some difference, etc. I soon found the advantage of this change in my manner; the conversations I engaged in went on more pleasantly. The modest way in which I proposed my opinions procured them a readier reception and less contradiction; I had less mortification when I was found to be in the wrong, and I more easily prevailed with others to give up their mistakes and join with me when I happened to be in the right. . . .

In reality there is, perhaps, no one of our natural passions so hard to subdue as Pride. Disguise it, struggle with it, beat it down, stifle it, mortify it as much as one pleases, it is still alive, and will every now and then peep out and show itself; you will see it, perhaps, often in this history; for even if I could conceive that I had completely overcome it, I should probably be proud of my humility.

| *"You're never going to get it all together.'*
There isn't going to be some precious
future time when all the loose ends will be
tied up."

Abandon Any Hope of Fruition

Pema Chödrön

American Buddhist nun Pema Chödrön is the resident
teacher at Gampo Abbey, in Cape Breton, Nova Scotia, the
first Tibetan Buddhist monastery in North America established for Westerners. In the following viewpoint Chödrön
maintains that people should abandon projects of self-
improvement and accept themselves as they are at present.
The belief that we can work to become better or more enlightened orients us to the future and causes us to neglect
what we already have, Chödrön contends. But when we unconditionally accept ourselves as we are, flaws and all, we develop a deeper compassion for human nature and can approach life with an open heart and an open mind.

As you read, consider the following questions:
1. What is one of the most powerful teachings in the
   Buddhist tradition, according to Chödrön?
2. What does it mean to be a grown-up, in Chödrön's
   opinion?
3. According to Zen master Bodhidharma, cited by the
   author, what is enlightenment?

[O]ne important teaching] is "Abandon any hope of fruition." You could also say, "Give up all hope" or "Give up" or just "Give." The shorter the better.

One of the most powerful teachings of the Buddhist tradition is that as long as you are wishing for things to change, they never will. As long as you're wanting yourself to get better, you won't. As long as you have an orientation toward the future, you can never just relax into what you already have or already are.

One of the deepest habitual patterns that we have is to feel that now is not good enough. We think back to the past a lot, which maybe was better than now, or perhaps worse. We also think ahead quite a bit to the future—which we may fear—always holding out hope that it might be a little bit better than now. Even if now is going really well—we have good health and we've met the person of our dreams, or we just had a child or got the job we wanted—nevertheless there's a deep tendency always to think about how it's going to be later. We don't quite give ourselves full credit for who we are in the present.

For example, it's easy to hope that things will improve as a result of meditation, that we won't have such bad tempers anymore or we won't have fear anymore or people will like us more than they do now. Or maybe none of those things are problems for us, but we feel we aren't spiritual enough. Surely we will connect with that awake, brilliant, sacred world that we are going to find through meditation. In everything we read—whether it's philosophy or dharma books or psychology—there's the implication that we're caught in some kind of very small perspective and that if we just did the right things, we'd begin to connect with a bigger world, a vaster world, different from the one we're in now.

You Will Never Get It Together

One reason I wanted to talk about giving up all hope of fruition is because I've been meditating and giving dharma talks for some time now, but I find that I still have a secret passion for what it's going to be like when—as they say in some of the classical texts—"all the veils have been removed." It's that same feeling of wanting to jump over yourself and find something that's more awake than the present situation, more alert than the present situation. Sometimes this occurs at a very mundane level: you want to be thinner, have less acne or more hair. But somehow there's almost always a subtle or not so subtle sense of disappointment, a sense of things not completely measuring up.

In one of the first teachings I ever heard, the teacher said, "I don't know why you came here, but I want to tell you right now that the basis of this whole teaching is that you're never going to get everything together." I felt a little like he had just slapped me in the face or thrown cold water over my head. But I've always remembered it. He said, "You're never going to get it all together." There isn't going to be some precious future time when all the loose ends will be tied up. Even though it was shocking to me, it rang true. One of the things that keeps us unhappy is this continual searching for pleasure or security, searching for a little more comfortable situation, either at the domestic level or at the spiritual level or at the level of mental peace.

Nowadays, people go to a lot of different places trying to find what they're looking for. There are 12-step programs; someone told me that there is now a 24-step program; someday there will probably be a 108-step program. There are a lot of support groups and different therapies. Many people feel wounded and are looking for something to heal them. To me it seems that at the root of healing, at the root of feeling like a fully adult person, is the premise that you're not going to try to make anything go away, that what you have is worth appreciating. But this is hard to swallow if what you have is pain.

Break the "Not Good Enough" Pattern

In Boston there's a stress-reduction clinic run on Buddhist principles. It was started by Dr. Jon Kabat-Zinn, a Buddhist practitioner and author of *Full Catastrophe Living*. He says that the basic premise of his clinic—to which many people come with a lot of pain—is to give up any hope of fruition. Otherwise the treatment won't work. If there's some sense of wanting to change yourself, then it comes from a place of feeling that you're not good enough. It comes from aggression toward yourself, dislike of your present mind, speech, or body; there's something about yourself that you feel is not good enough. People come to the clinic with addictions, abuse issues, or stress from work—with all kinds of issues. Yet this simple ingredient of giving up hope is the most important ingredient for developing sanity and healing.

"We thought it was a rough patch, but it turned out to be our life."

Kaplan. © 2003 by The Cartoon Bank. Reproduced by permission.

That's the main thing. As long as you're wanting to be thinner, smarter, more enlightened, less uptight, or whatever it might be, somehow you're always going to be approaching your problem with the very same logic that created it to begin with: you're not good enough. That's why the habitual pattern never unwinds itself when you're trying to improve, because you go about it in exactly the same habitual style that caused all the pain to start [with].

Compassion for Our Inherent Nature

There's a life-affirming teaching in Buddhism, which is that Buddha, which means "awake," is not someone you worship. Buddha is not someone you aspire to; Buddha is not somebody that was born more than two thousand years ago and was smarter than you'll ever be. Buddha is our inherent nature—our buddha nature—and what that means is that if you're going to grow up fully, the way that it happens is that you begin to connect with the intelligence that you already have. It's not like some intelligence that's going to be transplanted into you. If you're going to be fully mature, you will no longer be imprisoned in the childhood feeling that you always need to protect yourself or shield yourself because things are too harsh. If you're going to be a grown-up—which I would define as being completely at home in your world no matter how difficult the situation—it's because you will allow something that's already in you to be nurtured. You allow it to grow, you allow it to come out, instead of all the time shielding it and protecting it and keeping it buried.

Someone once told me, "When you feel afraid, that's 'fearful buddha.'" That could be applied to whatever you feel. Maybe anger is your thing. You just go out of control and you see red, and the next thing you know you're yelling or throwing something or hitting someone. At that time, begin to accept the fact that that's "enraged buddha." If you feel jealous, that's "jealous buddha." If you have indigestion, that's "buddha with heartburn." If you're happy, "happy buddha"; if bored, "bored buddha." In other words, anything that you can experience or think is worthy of compassion; anything you could think or feel is worthy of appreciation.

This teaching was powerful for me; it stuck. I would find myself in various states of mind and various moods, going up and down, going left and right, falling on my face and sitting up—just in all these different life situations—and I would remember, "Buddha falling flat on her face; buddha feeling on top of the world; buddha longing for yesterday." I began to learn that I couldn't get away from buddha no matter how hard I tried. I could stick with myself through thick and thin. If one would enter into an unconditional relationship with oneself, one would be entering into an unconditional relationship with buddha.

An Unconditional Relationship with Yourself

This is why the slogan says, "Abandon any hope of fruition." "Fruition" implies that at a future time you will feel good.

There is another word, which is *open*—to have an open heart and open mind. This is oriented very much to the present. If you enter into an unconditional relationship with yourself, that means sticking with the buddha right now on the spot as you find yourself.

Because it's a monastery, there's nothing you can do at Gampo Abbey that's fun, unless you like to meditate all the time or take walks in nature, but everything gets boring after awhile. There's no sex there, you can't drink there, you also can't lie. Occasionally we'll see a video, but that's rare and usually there's a dispute about what it's going to be. The food is sometimes good and sometimes terrible; it's just a very uncomfortable place. The reason it's uncomfortable is that you can't get away from yourself there. However, the more people make friends with themselves, the more they find it a nurturing and supportive place where you can find out the buddhaness of your own self as you are right now, today. Right now today, could you make an unconditional relationship with yourself? Just at the height you are, the weight you are, the amount of intelligence that you have, the burden of pain that you have? Could you enter into an unconditional relationship with that?

Be Awake in the Present Moment

Giving up any hope of fruition has something in common with the title of my . . . book, *The Wisdom of No Escape*. "No escape" leaves you continually right in the present, and the present is whatever it is, whatever mood you happen to be in, whatever thoughts you happen to be having. That's it.

Whether you get meditation instruction from the Theravada tradition or the Zen tradition or the Vajrayana tradition, the basic instruction is always about being awake in the present moment. What they don't tell you is that the present moment can be you, this you about whom you sometimes don't feel very good. That's what there is to wake up to.

When one of the emperors of China asked Bodhidharma (the Zen master who brought Zen from India to China) what enlightenment was, his answer was, "Lots of space, nothing holy." Meditation is nothing holy. Therefore there's nothing that you think or feel that somehow gets put in the category of "sin." There's nothing that you can think or feel that gets put in the category of "bad." There's nothing that you can think or feel that gets put in the category of "wrong." It's all good juicy stuff—the manure of waking up, the manure of achieving enlightenment, the art of living in the present moment.

For Further Discussion

Chapter 1

1. In his viewpoint M. Scott Peck discusses transference, which he defines as the inappropriate application of a childhood view of the world to the adult environment. He also speculates on the role transference may play in community and international relationships—such as how Americans' experiences during the 1930s and 1940s may have influenced the way American leaders waged war in Vietnam. Do you see possible examples of transference in national and international affairs today? What are they? Do you think that today's world leaders may be influenced by their childhood ways of perceiving and responding to the world? Why or why not?

2. Imagine that Plato visited you and addressed his allegory of the cave to you directly, with the cave being a description of your life and your world. What insights would his allegory give you? In your life situation, what might the terms "shadows," "light," "ascent," and "sight" symbolize?

3. M. Scott Peck uses the image of the map, Plato uses the metaphor of the cave, and Sam Keen uses the idea of myth to help people better understand their lives and the nature of truth. Which metaphor do you believe provides the best guidance for constructing a life philosophy? Explain.

4. Charles Larmore challenges the common philosophical notion that "the life lived well is the life lived in accord with a rational plan." In your opinion, does Larmore's viewpoint negate or enhance the concept of constructing a life philosophy? Use citations from the chapter as you compose your answer.

Chapter 2

1. Richard Robinson rejects the existence of God. For this reason he concludes that we must create our own purpose in life and "behave brotherly to each other" in light of humanity's insecurity and inevitable extinction. George E. Saint-Laurent maintains that religious believers often commune with the sacred by dying to self, giving alms, and serving the needy. In your opinion, does Robinson's atheistic humanism provide a more solid foundation than religion for promoting human welfare? Why or why not?

2. Wayne Anderson argues that science is preferable to religion in pursuing the meaning of life. Sharon Begley maintains that both

science and religion can illuminate the mysteries of the cosmos. What supporting arguments do the authors use to back up their conclusions? On what points do they agree? On what points do they disagree? In the end, whose argument do you find more compelling? Use evidence from the text as you explain your answer.

Chapter 3

1. Judaism is the ancestor of both Christianity and Islam. After reading this chapter, identify the elements that these three belief systems share. Then examine what features distinguish them. How do these religions differ in their approaches to faith membership, scripture, the nature of God, social justice, and the ultimate goal of life?

2. Donald E. Miller and Bob George present contrasting views on how Christians should interpret the Bible. What supportive arguments does each author use to back up his conclusion? Which author's approach to interpreting scripture do you prefer? Why?

3. Compare and contrast the Hindu conception of God and the Buddhist ideal of enlightenment. What role do spiritual disciplines and wise teachers play for Hindus and Buddhists on the path to ultimate reality?

4. How do Riane Eisler and Wayne Teasdale envision humanity's future? Do you believe that these authors are overly idealistic, or do you see evidence in the world today that their hopes could come to fruition? Explain.

Chapter 4

1. Philip Yancey maintains that without the guidance of religion, people have no way of distinguishing between right and wrong. Do you agree with his argument that religion is the only reliable guide to determining what is right and wrong? What alternative view does Frank R. Zindler propose?

2. Paul Kurtz argues that secular humanism provides a "method for the explanation and discovery of rational moral principles." How do you think John Gray would respond to Kurtz's assertion? Which author's argument do you think is more convincing? Cite passages from the viewpoints to support your conclusions.

3. After reading the viewpoints by Alfie Kohn and Tibor R. Machan, what are your thoughts about the psychological motivations for helping others? Do you agree with Kohn that the desire to benefit others is largely rooted in altruism, or do you accept Machan's belief that truly moral actions begin with self-interest?

Or do you think that both altruism and self-interest prompt moral behavior? Give specific examples to support your claim.

Chapter 5

1. Robert Ringer argues that our goal in life should be to spend as much time as possible pursuing those things that bring us pleasure and less time on those that cause pain. Ole Hallesby contends that people should live as Jesus Christ did by serving others and even by sacrificing one's self for others. How might each author respond to Niccolò Machiavelli's warning that we must constantly be on guard to protect ourselves because most people are selfish and untrustworthy?

2. Benjamin Franklin discusses how he decided to develop and follow a systematic program to reach moral perfection. While he was unsuccessful, he believes that his attempts at perfection made him a better person. Conversely, Pema Chödrön urges readers to abandon hopes of becoming better in the future, arguing that the continual search for improvement is a kind of illusion that takes us out of the realities of the present moment. Although these writers are from different centuries and promote seemingly opposing philosophies, are there any supporting ideas that they share in common? Can Franklin's musings on humility and pride be compared with Chödrön's assertion that we should unconditionally accept ourselves? Why or why not?

Bibliography

Reading the full texts from which the viewpoints in this anthology were taken is highly recommended. In addition to those texts, the following works and Web sites are recommended for further study.

Books

Peter Angeles, ed.
Critiques of God. New York: Prometheus, 1976. Seventeen thinkers present a variety of arguments against belief in God.

Phillip L. Berman, ed.
The Courage of Conviction. New York: Ballantine, 1986. Thirty-three prominent people reveal their beliefs and how they act on them.

Swami Bhaskarananda
The Essentials of Hinduism: A Comprehensive Overview of the World's Oldest Religion. Seattle, WA: Viveka Press, 2002. A clearly written explanation of the basic ideas and practices of Hinduism.

Frederic and Mary Ann Brussat
Spiritual Literacy: Reading the Sacred in Everyday Life. New York: Scribner, 1996. The authors present hundreds of brief discussions about daily life from spiritual teachers, writers, artists, filmmakers, naturalists, and social activists.

Wayne D. Dosick
Living Judaism: The Complete Guide to Jewish Belief, Tradition, and Practice. San Francisco: HarperSanFrancisco, 1998. A straightforward introduction to Judaism.

Riane Eisler
The Chalice and the Blade. New York: Harper & Row, 1987. Eisler argues that a partnership model of society, rooted in goddess worship, is the true foundation of civilization.

Clifton Fadiman, ed.
Living Philosophies. New York: Doubleday, 1990. Thirty-six eminent men and women express their ultimate beliefs and doubts.

Robert Frager
The Wisdom of Islam: A Practical Guide to the Wisdom of Islamic Belief. Hauppauge, NY: Barron's Educational Series, 2002. A Muslim convert provides a basic introduction to the history and tenets of Islam.

Bob George
Classic Christianity. Eugene, OR: Harvest House, 1989. The author presents an easy-to-read survey of traditional Christian beliefs.

Stephen Jay Gould
Rocks of Ages: Science and Religion in the Fullness of Life. New York: Ballantine, 2002. A renowned evolutionist argues that while science and reli-

gion cannot be unified, they need not be in conflict.

Thich Nhat Hanh	*The Heart of the Buddha's Teaching.* New York: Broadway Books, 1999. A scholar, poet, and monk presents the core teachings of Buddhism.
Arnold D. Hunt, Robert B. Crotty, and Marie T. Crotty, eds.	*Ethics of World Religions.* San Diego: Greenhaven, 1991. An examination of ethical issues from the point of view of various world religions.
William Johnston	*"Arise, My Love . . .": Mysticism for a New Era.* Maryknoll, NY: Orbis Books, 2000. A Jesuit priest offers an overview of the dialogue between Christian mysticism and Eastern religious traditions.
Paul Kurtz	*Eupraxophy: Living Without Religion.* New York: Prometheus Books, 1989. One of America's foremost advocates of humanism outlines his theory that one can lead a good and ethical life without the practice of religion.
Corliss Lamont	*The Philosophy of Humanism.* New York: Continuum, 1990. A former honorary president of the American Humanist Association presents a classic explanation and defense of humanism.
Michael Lerner	*Spirit Matters: Global Healing and the Wisdom of the Soul.* Charlottesville, VA: Hampton Roads, 2000. A rabbi discusses how spiritual meaning can be woven into the fabric of a pluralistic society.
David Mills	*Atheist Universe: Why God Didn't Have a Thing to Do with It.* Philadelphia: Xlibris, 2004. The author maintains that God is unnecessary to explain the universe and life's diversity, organization, and beauty.
Kristen Renwick Monroe	*The Heart of Altruism.* Princeton, NJ: Princeton University Press, 1998. The author examines why altruism emerges and demonstrates how social science theories can account for altruism.
Diarmuid O'Murchu	*Quantum Theology: Spiritual Implications of the New Physics.* New York: Crossroads, 1997. A priest and social psychologist presents a theology that embraces the latest advances in quantum physics.
J.B. Phillips	*Your God Is Too Small.* New York: Macmillan, 1961. The author suggests that most people do not grasp the true nature of God. If they truly understood God, Phillips believes, they would be more open to religion.

Ayn Rand	*The Virtue of Selfishness: A New Concept of Egoism.* New York: Signet, 1961. A discussion of objectivist philosophy and an ethics based on rational self-interest.
Carl Sagan	*The Demon-Haunted World: Science as a Candle in the Dark.* New York: Random House, 1995. Sagan, a scientist and popular author, explains how science is the best means for humans to understand themselves and the world.
John Shelby Spong	*A New Christianity for a New World: Why Traditional Faith Is Dying and How a New Faith Is Being Born.* San Francisco: HarperSanFrancisco, 2002. An Episcopalian bishop makes the case for a progressive and nontheistic Christianity.
Ken Wilber	*A Theory of Everything.* Boston: Shambhala, 2000. A renowned contemporary philosopher presents a vision of the world that includes body, mind, soul, and spirit as they appear in self, culture, and nature.
Alan Wolfe	*Moral Freedom: The Search for Virtue in a World of Choice.* New York: Free Press, 2002. Diverse Americans are questioned about their views on loyalty, honesty, self-restraint, and forgiveness.

Web Sites

Atheism	Americanatheist.org. An online version of *American Atheist*, a quarterly magazine of atheist news and thought.
Buddhism	Tricycle.com. A site sponsored by *Tricycle*, a magazine that promotes Buddhism in the United States.
Christianity	Christianitytoday.com. This site is sponsored by *Christianity Today* magazine and offers a wide range of links to discussions and ideas presented from a traditional Protestant perspective.
	Tcpc.org. The Center for Progressive Christianity provides resources for progressive churches, organizations, individuals, and others with connections to Christianity.
Ecofeminism	Ecofem.org. This site includes general information on ways to unify feminism and ecology.
Ethics	Josephsoninstitute.org. This is a secular, nonpartisan organization dedicated to cultivating the study and practice of "principled reasoning and ethical decision making."

Hinduism	Hinduwebsite.com. This site provides comprehensive information on Hinduism and related religions.
Humanism	Humanist.net. Sponsored by the American Humanist Association and *Humanist* magazine, this site provides a forum for ideas from a humanist perspective.
Islam	Islamworld.net. This site offers an introduction to Islam for non-Muslims, with links to articles on Islamic beliefs and practices.
Judaism	Jewfaq.org. This Web site includes "Judaism 101," an online encyclopedia covering Jewish beliefs, people, practices, and customs.
Mysticism and World Religions	Digiserve.com/mystic. This site presents an introduction to comparative mysticism, with links to articles about the world's mystical traditions.
Philosophy	Plato.stanford.edu. The Stanford Encyclopedia of Philosophy provides an alphabetized archive with links to detailed articles on philosophical concepts, history, and theories.
Science and Religion	Thegreatstory.org. This educational Web site promotes "the marriage of science and the sacred for personal and planetary well-being."

Index

234

237